First Dinosaur Encyclopedia

REVISED EDITION
US Editor Margaret Parrish
Assistant editor Debangana Banerjee
Assistant art editor Kartik Gera
Project editor Suneha Dutta
Senior editor Shatarupa Chaudhuri
DTP designer Bimlesh Tiwary
Managing editors Laura Gilbert,
Alka Thakur Hazarika
Managing art editors Diane Peyton Jones,
Romi Chakraborty
Producer Nicole Landau
Senior producer, pre-production Ben Marcus
Publisher Sarah Larter
Publishing director Sophie Mitchell
Art director Stuart Jackman
CTS manager Balwant Singh
Publisher Sarah Larter
Jacket editor Ishani Nandi
Jacket designer Kartik Gera
Consultant John Woodward

ORIGINAL EDITION
Written and edited by Caroline Bingham
Design team Jane Tetzlaff, Tory Gordon-Harris,
Clare Harris, Claire Patane, Mary Sandberg,
Helen Chapman, Kath Northam
Art editor Rachael Foster
Consultant Dougal Dixon B.SC. (Hons.), M.SC
Publishing Manager Sue Leonard
Jacket Designer Karen Hood
Picture Researcher Liz Moore
Production Controller Lucy Baker
DTP Designer Emma Hansen-Knarhoi
Category Publisher Mary Ling
DK Picture Library Rose Horridge, Claire Bowers

This American Edition, 2016
First American Edition, 2006
Published in the United States by DK Publishing
1450 Broadway, Suite 801, New York, NY 10018

Copyright © 2006, © 2016 Dorling Kindersley Limited
DK, a Division of Penguin Random House LLC
19 20 21 10 9 8 7 6 5
011—280450—Jun/2016

A catalog record for this title is available from the Library of Congress.
ISBN 978-1-4654-4346-5

DK books are available at special discounts when purchased in bulk for
sales promotions, premiums, fund-raising, or educational use. For details,
contact: DK Publishing Special Markets,
1450 Broadway, Suite 801, New York, NY 10018
SpecialSales@dk.com.

Printed and bound in China

A WORLD OF IDEAS:
SEE ALL THERE IS TO KNOW

www.dk.com

Contents

Age of the dinosaurs

Let's look at dinosaurs

Triassic dinosaurs

There is a question at the bottom of each page...

About this book

The pages of this book have special features that will show you how to get your hands on as much information as possible! Look out for these:

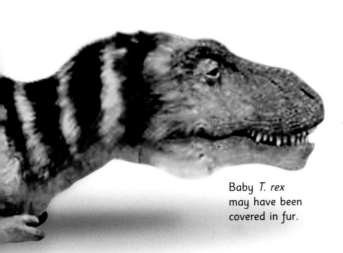

Baby *T. rex* may have been covered in fur.

The Picture Detective will get you searching through each section for the answers.

Turn and Learn tells you where to look for more information on a subject.

Every page is color-coded to show you which section it is in.

weird or what? These buttons give extra weird and wonderful facts.

Age of the dinosaurs

The Earth has an incredibly long history, because it formed about 4.6 billion years ago. Geologists divide the passage of time since into huge chunks called eras. The giant dinosaurs lived in the Mesozoic Era.

Eoraptor was a Triassic dinosaur.

A question of time

Different dinosaurs lived at different times, and many of the best-known dinosaurs never actually met. For example, no *T. rex* ever tried to kill a *Stegosaurus* because their existence was separated by about 80 million years.

MESOZOIC ERA

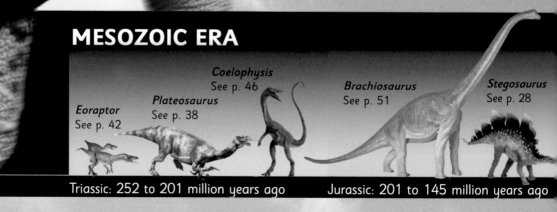

Coelophysis
See p. 46

Plateosaurus
See p. 38

Eoraptor
See p. 42

Brachiosaurus
See p. 51

Stegosaurus
See p. 28

Triassic: 252 to 201 million years ago   Jurassic: 201 to 145 million years ago

4

How do we know what dinosaurs looked like?

Picture detective
Look through the Age of the Dinosaurs pages to identify each of the picture clues below.

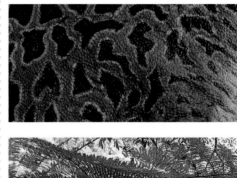

The Mesozoic Era
This era is divided into three time spans, or periods.

The **Cretaceous** period was ruled by an amazing variety of dinosaurs.

The **Jurassic** period saw the emergence of massive plant-eating dinosaurs.

The **Triassic** period, the oldest, saw the appearance of the Earth's first dinosaurs.

Geological time is always shown with the oldest period at the bottom of the list. It reflects the sequence in which rocks are laid down.

Giganotosaurus
See p. 78

Velociraptor
See p. 84

T. rex
See p. 76

Human beings (*Homo sapiens*) didn't appear until very recently in the Earth's history.

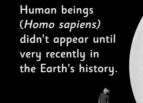

Cretaceous: 145 to 66 million years ago   *Homo sapiens*

Turn and learn
Where *Albertosaurus* roamed:
pp. 68–69

We know a lot about their size and appearance from fossil evidence.

The "terrible lizard"

Prof. Richard Owen (1804–1892) with the skeleton of a moa, an extinct flightless bird.

Scientists once believed dinosaur fossils were the bones of a type of lizard. In fact, the word "dinosaur" means "terrible lizard." It was first used in 1841.

A starting point

When Richard Owen first coined the term "dinosaur," only three of the creatures had been identified: *Iguanodon*, *Megalosaurus*, and *Hylaeosaurus*.

Lizard

It's the same one!

Is it two-footed or four? Where does that spiked part go? Ideas about dinosaurs change over the years, as these portrayals of *Iguanodon* show.

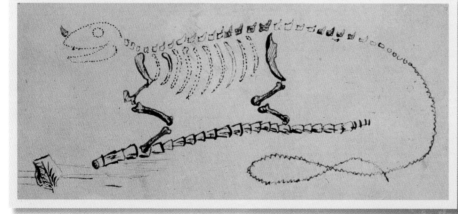

The first sketch of *Iguanodon* had a spike positioned on its snout.

Was *Iguanodon* a plant-eater or a meat-eater?

Where in the world?

From sparse beginnings, dinosaurs have now been found on every continent, including the now frozen Antarctica. This map gives an idea of where just a few dinosaur remains have been found.

Europe: *Iguanodon, Baryonyx, Plateosaurus*

North America: *Stegosaurus, Apatosaurus, Triceratops*

Asia: *Velociraptor, Protoceratops, Mamenchisaurus*

Africa: *Spinosaurus, Barosaurus*

South America: *Saltasaurus, Argentinosaurus*

Antarctica: *Glacialisaurus, Hypsilophodon*

Australia/New Zealand: *Rhoetosaurus, Minmi, Muttaburrasaurus*

In the 1850s, a sculpture of *Iguanodon* showed a lizard crawling on its belly.

The name *Iguanodon* means "iguana toothed." The teeth were like those of the iguana, the modern, plant-eating lizard.

Turn and learn

What a dinosaur is: **pp. 14-15**

We now know that *Iguanodon* had spikes on its thumbs, not on its nose.

Scientists believe that *Iguanodon* could walk on four feet, as well as on two.

It was a plant-eater.

A very different Earth

The Earth is constantly changing. Today there are seven continents, but the first dinosaurs lived on one giant supercontinent called Pangaea.

A moving jigsaw

The Earth's crust is made up of sections, called plates, which are always on the move. Continents rest on the plates. Over time, this movement changes the shape of the land.

Triassic period

It's breaking up

During the late Triassic period, Pangaea began to break up to form two supercontinents. By the end of the Cretaceous period, the landmasses had undergone huge changes. From space, the Earth would have looked more like it does today, with large continents separated by gigantic oceans.

Pangaea   Panthalassa

The Triassic period saw the world's land all joined together as a supercontinent.

What are the names of the Earth's seven continents?

We're free to roam
The existence of one huge landmass meant that in the early- to mid-Triassic period animals and plants were similar throughout the world.

Pangaea means "All Earth."

What was different?
Pangaea's world had no ice caps and the land was hot and dry; large areas of desert dominated the center of this vast continent.

Jurassic period

Laurasia

Tethys sea

Gondwana

The landmass split apart in the Jurassic period, forming two huge continents.

Cretaceous period

South America

Africa

India

Antarctica

The landmasses we know today began to appear during the Cretaceous period.

9

What did they see?

The dinosaurs looked out onto a very different world from the one we see today. It was a world without roads, houses, parks, and all the machines humans use. So what was it like?

Habitat
Like us, the dinosaurs lived in different habitats. A habitat is an area that animals and plants share. It may be a desert or a busy city street.

Iguanodon was a plant-eater. By the time *Iguanodon* lived, the first flowering plants had appeared.

How many different types of grass are there today?

From Triassic forests...

The first dinosaurs saw only brown and green plants—there were no flowers. Giant forests contained trees that were similar to plants we know today, only larger.

Triassic scene

Cycad

Ginkgo leaves

Monkey puzzle

Horsetail

... to Cretaceous flowers

The first flowering plants, such as magnolias and passion flowers, appeared in the Cretaceous period. By the late Cretaceous, there were also buttercups.

Magnolia

Fossilized dinosaur dung (coprolite)

Fossilized grass remains were found in dinosaur dung.

What about grass?

Until recently, scientists believed grass evolved after the dinosaurs, but there's now proof that some dinosaurs did eat grass. And it may have been grass that was several yards tall!

Buttercup

Dinosaur habitats

The dinosaurs enjoyed a huge variety of habitats, including those below.

 Large areas of **desert** were common in the Mesozoic Era.

 Trees in Triassic **forests** were protected from over-browsing by tough needles.

 Mountains increasingly appeared in the Mesozoic Era.

 Scrublands were huge areas of scrubby, drought-resistant plants.

 Cretaceous **swamps** were good places for fossil preservation.

Triassic dinosaurs stayed close to coasts or **riverbanks**.

Let's look at dinosaurs

Sauropods, such as *Barosaurus*, were the largest land animals ever.

Barosaurus

Large... small... meat-eater... plant-eater... There was an incredible variety of dinosaurs and we will probably never know just how many different kinds there were.

T. rex was a large theropod.

I've got that!

Dinosaurs had plenty of features in common.

Scaly skin, and feathers in some cases, covered the bodies of dinosaurs.

Long tails were used for balance and as whips to fight off enemies.

Legs were held straight under the body.

Whether meat-eater (theropod) or plant-eater (sauropod), all had **claws**.

T. rex

Lesothosaurus

The very first dinosaurs, such as *Lesothosaurus*, were all small. Larger dinosaurs, such as *Stegosaurus*, came later.

12

How long did dinosaurs live?

How many dinosaurs?

Scientists think there may have been at least 1,500 different dinosaur types, and probably many more. We know of about 800 that can be confirmed as distinct types, so there are many more to discover.

Sauropods

Pentaceratops

Pentaceratops means "five-horned face."

How are they named?

Dinosaurs are usually named after the person who found them, after their features, or after the place where they were found.

Turn and learn

T. rex:
pp. 76-77
Triceratops:
pp. 72-73

Stegosaurus

T. rex: pp. 76-77 Triceratops: pp. 72-73

Picture detective

Look through the Let's Look at Dinosaurs pages to identify each of the picture clues below.

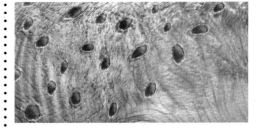

No one knows. Some may have lived for 80 years.

What is a dinosaur?

Two legs or four? Meat-eater or plant-eater? What made a dinosaur? They all had four limbs, though many walked on two. There were a number of other features they had in common.

Long tails
Scientists believe dinosaurs held their tails above the ground because there is no evidence of drag marks where trackways have been found.

Scaly skin
Impressions of dinosaur skin are rare, but paleontologists have found enough to know that many dinosaurs had scaly skin, a bit like lizards today.

Cold-blooded lizards have to warm up in sunlight; they cannot control their temperature.

Were dinosaurs warm-blooded?
It's likely that the meat-eating dinosaurs were warm-blooded, like us, but scientists are not sure if the biggest plant-eaters were, too. Warm-blooded animals use food as fuel to stay warm, so the giant plant-eaters may not have managed to eat enough to do this.

Meat-eating dinosaurs, such as *Giganotosaurus*, were known as theropods.

14

Are dinosaurs lizards?

Giganotosaurus skulls had huge "windows."

Skull holes

Dinosaur skulls had large holes, or "windows." These made them lighter, which was necessary as some of the largest skulls were almost as long as a car.

Meat-eaters had sharp claws.

Plant-eaters had blunt toenails.

Clue in the claws

Meat-eating dinosaurs were known as theropods, which means "beast-footed," because they had sharp, hooked claws on their toes. Plant-eating dinosaurs (sauropods) tended to have blunt hooves or toenails.

Walking tall

Dinosaurs walked on their toes with their legs directly under their bodies.

Dinosaurs walked on upright, pillarlike legs.

Crocodiles stand with their knees and elbows slightly bent.

Lizards sprawl, with their knees and elbows held at right angles to their bodies.

Egg layers

All dinosaurs laid eggs—some in nests, just as birds do today. The baby developed in the egg until it was ready to hatch. About 40 kinds of dinosaur eggs have been discovered.

15

No. They are related, but the two groups are different.

A hip question

Dinosaurs can be split into two groups, according to their hip bones: the saurischians (lizard-hipped) and the ornithischians (bird-hipped).

Most lizard-hipped dinosaurs had a pair of hip bones that pointed forward or down.

Bird-hipped dinosaurs had two pairs of hip bones pointing back.

Did *T. rex* and *Triceratops* ever meet?

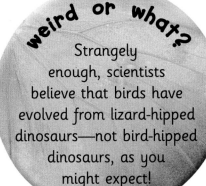

T. rex

Triceratops

Saurischians

All meat-eating dinosaurs were lizard-hipped, but some plant-eaters were also lizard-hipped. *T. rex* was lizard-hipped, but so was the mighty plant-eating *Diplodocus*, whom you will meet on page 50.

I'm in this group!

Saurischians can be divided into two main groups.

Theropods, the meat-eaters, such as *Dilophosaurus*.

Sauropodomorphs, such as *Brachiosaurus*, with their small heads and long necks.

Ornithischians

These were all plant-eaters. The swept-back bones allowed more room for the digestive organs; because of this, their bellies were carried toward the back. This made them stable, and allowed them to run from danger on two legs.

I'm in that group!

Ornithischians can be divided into three main groups.

Thyreophorans, the four-footed, armor-plated dinosaurs (e.g., *Stegosaurus*).

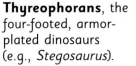

Marginocephalians, who had heads with bony frills or horns (e.g., *Triceratops*).

Ornithopods, the two-legged plant-eaters (e.g., *Iguanodon*).

17

Yes. There's evidence that *T. rex* preyed on *Triceratops*.

From little to big

Not all dinosaurs were giants, as is often believed. The smaller dinosaurs, such as *Oviraptor*, would have barely reached the large plant-eaters' ankles!

Long in the tooth?
Like humans, most dinosaurs had teeth.

Human molars are used for grinding food before it is swallowed.

Ankylosaurs had small, ridged teeth for slicing up plant matter.

Sauropods had long, peglike teeth.

Thighbone from a *Brachiosaurus*

Big head
It's difficult to imagine how large dinosaurs grew. Just look at this picture of a fossilized skull from a dinosaur that roamed the Sahara Desert 90 million years ago.

Carcharodontosaurus skull from the mid-Cretaceous period

From small...
Some dinosaurs are best described as tiny, such as the rabbit-sized *Micropachycephalosaurus*. Its lengthy name means "tiny, thick-headed lizard."

Micropachycephalosaurus

... to dog-sized...
The meat-eating *Oviraptor* was about 6 ft 6 in (2 m) from snout to tail. This dinosaur had an oddly shaped toothless beak.

Oviraptor lived in the Gobi Desert in Mongolia about 80 million years ago.

Which were the biggest dinosaurs?

Antarctosaurus

**Turn
and learn**
Oviraptor:
p. 23
Sauropods:
pp. 50–53

Antarctosaurus had an
immensely long neck,
which helped it to feed
high in the treetops.

... to truck-sized

The large plant-eaters,
the sauropods, were massive.
Antarctosaurus was about
60 ft (18 m) long and would
have towered over you. Other
plant-eaters may have been
larger still. Experts believe
that large sauropods ate
enough plants every day to
equal the weight of a small car.

Find a friend

Many male animals today compete to win a mate. Stags crash their antlers together, while birds display colorful feathers. Scientists believe dinosaurs had to compete in similar ways.

How did they court?

Dinosaurs may have used their head crests to show off, just like a peacock uses its colorful tail feathers.

Corythosaurus

Courtship displays tell females which males are strong and likely to make healthy young.

Peacock

Pachycephalosaurus

This dinosaur had bony spikes on its head and snout.

Bone head

Pachycephalosaurus's head was 2 ft 6 in (80 cm) long. The dome was made of solid bone as thick as a bowling ball.

Pachycephalosaurus skull

Fighting fit

During the breeding season, male *Pachycephalosaurus* may have butted each other in fights over females. Their thick skulls could have absorbed the impacts.

Where did *Pachycephalosaurus* live?

Did they talk?

No one knows if dinosaurs made sounds, but we suspect they did. *Parasaurolophus*, a hadrosaur (a duck-billed dinosaur), may have done this by blowing air through its crest.

Crest

Parasaurolophus skull

Lambeosaurus skull

Hypacrosaurus skull

Other hadrosaurs had different-shaped crests, suggesting they made different sounds.

Turn and learn
Crested hadrosaurs:
pp. 70-71

Parasaurolophus

Crest

Brachylophosaurus

Talk like a frog

Brachylophosaurus had a short, solid crest. It may have had an inflatable pouch on the outside of this that could be used to make noises, a little like a frog's throat pouch.

Throat pouch

Extraordinary eggs!

Scientists have been lucky enough to find lots of fossilized dinosaur eggs, and even nests. There is a huge variety of sizes and shapes—from small, circular eggs that would fit into the palm of your hand, to eggs the size of cannonballs.

Large scale
This massive egg was found in China and is thought to have been laid by a *Therizinosaurus*. There were larger eggs—the largest was laid by a dinosaur called *Macroelongatoolithus*.

This dinosaur egg fossil is from Mongolia.

A muddy home
Some eggs were laid in mud, which proved a perfect base for fossilization. These are *Maiasaura* eggs from Montana.

Many shapes
Some dinosaur eggs were round, but others were elongated, like a loaf of bread.

This is a hen's egg. It shows just how large the *Therizinosaurus* egg was.

Oviraptor nest from China, showing the eggs laid in a spiral pattern. Each egg is approximately 6 in (16 cm) long.

Were dinosaur egg shells soft and leathery like those of snakes?

I'm making a break for it!

A tiny dinosaur hatchling would break out of its egg casing. While some dinosaurs were probably ready to look after themselves after hatching, others would have depended on parental help for food and protection.

Model of *Parasaurolophus* hatchling

Fossilized
dinosaur egg

Citipati

Egg

Egg care?

Did dinosaurs sit on their eggs, like birds today? Some did; this *Citipati* died and was fossilized sitting on her eggs some 80 million years ago.

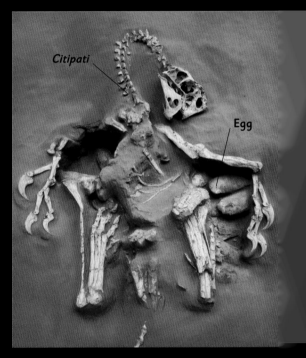

Turn and learn

Parental care of young dinosaurs:
pp. 24–25

Citipati

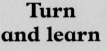

Nest is dug out of sand or soil.

Bringing it back to life

This model re-creates the fossilized scene above, showing the *Citipati* shielding her eggs. These dinosaurs had odd-looking beaked snouts. They may have raided other nests for food for themselves and their young.

No. They had hard, brittle shells, like the eggs of birds.

Birth and care of young

We know that some dinosaurs lived in colonies, thanks to finds of fossilized mud nests in Montana. These belonged to *Maiasaura*. The name means "good mother lizard."

Maiasaura

What a discovery!
Jack Horner was one of the paleontologists who discovered the nests in Montana. He's shown here with a fossilized nest.

Turn and learn

Dinosaurs that lived in groups: **pp. 30-31**

Let's look at the nests
The round nests were as wide as a car, 3 ft (1 m) high, and could hold 25 eggs. *Maiasaura* made their nests carefully, each creature forming a large mound with a hollow in it.

It's believed the nests were lined with vegetation.

What kind of dinosaur was *Maiasaura*?

Model of *Maiasaura* nest

Some hatchling fossils had worn teeth, suggesting they had been fed in the nest or had foraged and returned.

It's safer in the nest!

The nests contained trampled eggshells and some had bones of hatchlings, which suggests the young had remained in the nest after hatching. Similarly, many of today's birds remain in their nests until they can look after themselves.

I'm gonna grow!

The hatched babies weighed about as much as a big, heavy book and were about 1 ft (30 cm) long. The adult dinosaurs weighed as much as a small car and were as long as a bus.

We're hungry!

Experts don't think there were many plants around the nests, so the mothers probably found food elsewhere and brought it back to their young.

Colony life

The nests in Montana were spaced out, suggesting they were part of a colony. The spaces acted as pathways between nests and allowed the adults to lie next to the eggs to protect them.

It was a hadrosaur. Learn more about them on pages 70–71.

Hunting

Meat-eaters had to scavenge or hunt to stay alive. Some would have hunted alone, but there is also evidence of pack hunting. This does make it easier to corner and overcome prey. Just think how effective lions are at hunting today.

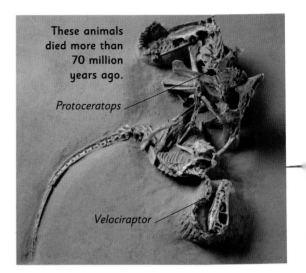

These animals died more than 70 million years ago.

Protoceratops

Velociraptor

A fight to the death
This amazing fossil captured the death throes of a *Protoceratops* and *Velociraptor* locked in combat. It provides proof that *Velociraptor* preyed on *Protoceratops*.

Fierce hunter
Velociraptor may only have been the size of a large dog, but it was probably an incredibly accomplished killer. Its narrow jaws contained bladelike fangs, and its fingers and toes were armed with daggerlike claws.

Velociraptor

Did dinosaurs ever hunt humans?

Let's join up

Scientists believe a number of dinosaurs may have hunted in packs.

Utahraptor was the largest known raptor. It prowled western America.

Deinonychus was a 10 ft (3 m) long killer that roamed North America.

Giganotosaurus was one of the largest meat-eaters.

Watch out! Rotten teeth!

Some of the large meat-eaters may have delivered a batch of bacteria when they bit. The largest living lizard, the Komodo dragon, has saliva full of bacteria that live on rotting meat stuck in its teeth. Its bite can poison its victim. The same may have applied to some of the dinosaurs.

Komodo dragon

A young *Protoceratops* would have had little chance of defending itself against a hungry *Velociraptor*.

Protoceratops

No. Humans appeared about 64 million years after the last dinosaurs.

Go away!

Plant-eating dinosaurs had to find ways to protect themselves against the sharp teeth and claws of meat-eaters. They tended to have tough skin—or armor—and some developed interesting weaponry.

Edmontonia lived in the same places and at the same time as *T. rex*, so it needed tough protection!

Walking shields

The armored dinosaurs, or ankylosaurs, were tanklike, with their low-to-the-ground appearance and heavily plated backs. There were many different kinds.

Chain-mail protection

Stegosaurus is instantly recognizable by its bony plates. It also had bony studs under its neck and on its hips, thighs, and tail. These were jointed like chain mail, preventing a meat-eater from biting, but allowing the *Stegosaurus* to move.

Stegosaurus

Could the ankylosaurs run away from danger?

Swing that club!

Ankylosaurus had a lump of thickened bone at the end of its tail, giving it a club shape. Its muscular tail would swing this club from side to side. It also had thick bone on its head, neck, and body.

Geysers shoot hot water into the air. They are rare today, but may have been more common in the Mesozoic Era.

Ankylosaurus has been described as a "living tank."

Ankylosaurus tail

Triceratops

Triceratops had a bony shield to protect its neck and shoulders.

Stay back!

Triceratops was one of the largest of all horned dinosaurs. It would have been an intimidating dinosaur to fight.

Tail defense

Tails—especially armored tails—were useful for swinging at predators.

Euoplocephalus had a club made from fused bone at the end of its tail.

Stegosaurus had spikes at the end of its tail that could be 3 ft (1 m) long.

Diplodocus may have used its long tail as a whip.

Scientists don't think they could run fast, so their body armor was their defense.

It's better with friends

Many of today's animals live in groups—some for protection (antelope) and some for hunting (lions). It is likely that many dinosaurs did the same, and for similar reasons.

Herd of *Iguanodon*

It's noisy here

Just imagine the sounds and clouds of dust as large groups of dinosaurs moved off. Herds of cattle can sound like thunder if they stampede. A herd of hefty dinosaurs must have been a jaw-dropping sight.

Large sauropods may have stuck together in big groups.

This way for food!

If dinosaurs did gather together in large groups, it suggests that some may have been migratory—they moved in search of fresh grazing, much as African wildebeest do today. Large plant-eating sauropods may have trekked massive distances.

30

How far would dinosaurs have migrated?

Being big and living in herds helps animals protect themselves from attack. Only the weak and young are picked off.

A dinosaur highway?

In Cretaceous times, an inland sea stretched from north to south through North America. Experts think that the beaches on the western side were used as a migration route, because masses of fossilized dinosaur footprints have been found there.

What's the proof?

Paleontologists use all sorts of evidence to determine which dinosaurs probably lived in herds.

Lots of bones from the same type of dinosaur are found in the same area.

Fossilized footprints show herds of particular dinosaurs moving together.

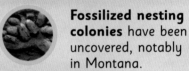

Fossilized nesting colonies have been uncovered, notably in Montana.

31

It is likely that some would migrate long distances of up to 185 miles (300 km).

Triassic dinosaurs

Just before the Triassic period, Earth suffered a mass extinction (probably caused by climate changes) that wiped out about 96 percent of all living things. It took millions of years before the planet began to recover.

Triassic Earth as it looked between 252 and 201 million years ago.

Animal life

Mammal-like reptiles of the early Triassic developed into true mammals by the end of the period.

Eozostrodon, one of the earliest true mammals, fed its young with milk.

Lystrosaurus, an early Triassic mammal-like reptile, was a dog-sized plant-eater.

Megazostrodon, a mammal, was about 5 in (12 cm) long. It may have eaten insects.

Eoraptor

What did the existence of one huge land mass mean for animal life?

So what was Earth like?

In Triassic times, the planet was hot and dry, with huge deserts. There were pockets of fertile land at the coasts, but there were no flowers. Earth would have been unrecognizable to us.

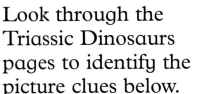

Herrerasaurus's body shape shows it would have been a fast-moving dinosaur.

Early dinosaurs would have seen huge areas of hot, red desert.

Herrerasaurus is one of the earliest known dinosaurs.

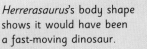

Staurikosaurus

New life appears

The Triassic period saw the gradual renewal of life on Earth, and the appearance of the largest creatures ever to roam there—the dinosaurs.

Picture detective

Look through the Triassic Dinosaurs pages to identify the picture clues below.

Turn and learn

Eoraptor:
pp. 42–43
Early mammals:
pp. 96–97

It meant that land animals were free to roam where they wanted.

The dinosaurs are coming

The name "archosaur" means "ruling lizard."

There were no dinosaurs at the start of the Triassic period. In fact, there was very little life. So where did they come from?

At the start

The dinosaurs were part of a group of reptiles called the archosaurs. One of the largest Triassic archosaurs was the formidable predator, *Postosuchus*.

Postosuchus grew to 15 ft (4.5 m) long.

An ancient history

Today's crocodiles are the biggest surviving archosaurs. Crocodiles have a similar body shape to the Triassic *Desmatosuchus*. Birds are also archosaurs.

Long shoulder spikes protected the animal's neck.

Desmatosuchus

Saltwater crocodile

34

Peteinosaurus

Early pterosaurs were not much larger than a modern crow.

Other archosaurs
Postosuchus was not the only archosaur, though it was the most fearsome.

Lagosuchus was just 1 ft (30 cm) in length.

Euparkeria was slightly larger, at 2 ft (60 cm) in length.

Chasmatosaurus reached lengths of 6 ft 6 in (2 m).

We were there!
Pterosaurs were flying reptiles, not dinosaurs, and they appeared in late Triassic skies. One of the first pterosaurs was *Peteinosaurus*.

Eudimorphodon

We are dinosaurs!
Some of the most primitive dinosaurs belong to a group called the coelurosaurs, a name that means "hollow-tailed reptile."

Coelophysis were just 6–10 ft (2–3 m) in length.

Bony plates covered *Desmatosuchus*'s back and tail, and part of its belly.

weird or what?
Although the mighty *T. rex* did not appear for another 160 million years, it was descended from the coelurosaurs.

No, but it was closely related.

Petrified Forest

The Petrified Forest in Arizona, North America, is packed with late Triassic fossils of plants and animals.

Not a dinosaur
The fossils in Arizona give us some idea of the sorts of animals that the first dinosaurs would have met. *Placerias* was a large reptile, growing up to 9 ft (2.7 m) long.

The trees were huge, originally standing at about 200 ft (60 m) in height.

Floodwaters covered the bases of the trees, uprooting many.

Placerias

Is that a crocodile?
Phytosaurs were crocodile-like reptiles. Some species grew as long as buses—up to 40 ft (12 m).

What dinosaur fossils have been found in the Petrified Forest?

Remains of a forest

Ancient fossilized trees dot the ground in the Petrified Forest. They are all that remain of a once mighty Triassic forest of conifer trees. So how have the trees been preserved for 220 million years?

Chindesaurus had particularly long hind legs.

Over millions of years, the trees were buried in gravelly sand. Gradually, they turned to stone.

Millions of years later the land eroded, exposing the fossilized trunks.

An early dinosaur

Chindesaurus is one of North America's earliest known dinosaurs. It could probably move fast when hunting.

37

Those of some of the world's first dinosaurs, such as *Chindesaurus* and *Coelophysis*.

Triassic plant-eaters

The Triassic saw the emergence of the prosauropods, an early type of sauropod (a dinosaur group that appeared later).

A long-named prosauropod

Thecodontosaurus was the first Triassic prosauropod to be named. It was a primitive plant-eating dinosaur with saw-edged teeth.

The first large dinosaur

Plateosaurus is believed to have been the first large dinosaur, reaching about 26 ft (8 m) in length. Scientists also think that it was one of the most common of the late Triassic dinosaurs.

Like most prosauropods, *Plateosaurus* was a plant-eater.

Turn and learn
Sauropods: pp. 50-55

Where have *Plateosaurus* fossils been found?

I can reach it!

Scientists think that *Plateosaurus* could stand on its back limbs to reach tree leaves. Fossils have been found in groups, suggesting it lived in herds.

The word "prosauropod" means "before sauropods."

Ginkgo leaves

Early dinosaurs had four- or five-fingered forelimbs.

Like later dinosaurs, *Plateosaurus* had large holes in its skull.

Prosauropods had long necks and tails but relatively small heads.

Plateosaurus

Teeth matter

Plateosaurus had small, leaf-shaped teeth set into its jaw. These helped it to shred tough leaves and stems.

Fossil of a *Mussaurus* hatchling

It's just a baby

Mussaurus, whose name means "mouse lizard," hatched from a tiny egg that was 1 in (2.5 cm) long, but grew to 10 ft (3 m) long.

Five-fingered forelimbs

France, Germany, and Switzerland.

From small beginnings

Early plant-eaters were small, but by the end of the Triassic, some grew to huge proportions.

Melanorosaurus

Riojasaurus

Lesothosaurus   Pisanosaurus

Mussaurus hatchling

Adult human

Melanorosaurus, or "black mountain lizard," was a bulky, four-footed plant-eater and possibly one of the first sauropods.

Don't get in the way!

Riojasaurus was a heavily built herbivore that grew to about 30–36 ft (9–11 m) in length. It had a long neck, body, and tail.

Riojasaurus

Dog-sized

Pisanosaurus was small, and the earliest known ornithishcian dinosaur. It probably fed on low-growing plants.

Pisanosaurus

Could *Riojasaurus* run?

It's so tiny!

Remember *Mussaurus*, which we met on page 39? Here you can see how this baby dinosaur's skull could fit on a fingertip. *Mussaurus* is the smallest fossilized dinosaur skeleton known. Large dinosaurs often started off small, but they grew and grew and grew.

When fully grown, a *Mussaurus* would have weighed some 260 lb (120 kg).

Turn and learn

What Triassic dinosaurs would have seen and eaten: **pp. 10-11**

Riojasaurus had spoon-shaped, serrated teeth.

Teeth talk

Riojasaurus would have used its teeth to pull needles and twigs from conifer trees. It may have swallowed them whole to be ground up in its stomach.

Plodding along

Riojasaurus moved slowly on thick, elephant-like legs. It probably lived in large herds for protection from predators.

Lesothosaurus

This small dinosaur appeared as the Triassic slipped into the Jurassic, making it one of the last Triassic dinosaurs. It lived on into the Jurassic.

Lesothosaurus

41

Yes, but it would have been unable to run very fast.

We're looking for meat!

As with today's animals, there were more plant-eaters than meat-eaters in the world of the dinosaurs. One of the earliest meat-eaters was the *Eoraptor*.

Old dinosaur bones

Just 3 ft (1 m) long, the fierce *Eoraptor* was only recently discovered and named when a near-complete skeleton was found in Argentina, South America, in 1991. The skeleton had been well-preserved.

Eoraptor's legs show it was probably a fast runner.

Hands and feet had sharp claws.

42

Staurikosaurus

This small meat-eater, or theropod, is another early dinosaur. It was a little bigger than *Eoraptor*, but still slender, and probably only the weight of a nine-year-old child.

Lightly built body

Four-fingered hands

Long thin tail used for balance

Eoraptor had large eyes, so probably enjoyed good vision.

Adult human

Eoraptor   *Staurikosaurus*

Staurikosaurus

We're ready to bite

Eoraptor probably ate lizards and small mammal-like reptiles, efficiently tearing into them with its sharp, curved front teeth.

Scientists believe *Eoraptor* lived 228 million years ago.

Dinosaur claws

As dinosaurs evolved, it seems that the number of fingers on their forelimbs decreased.

Four or five fingers were found on early dinosaurs, such as *Thecodontosaurus*.

Three fingers were found on later dinosaurs, such as *Allosaurus*.

Two fingers were found on many Cretaceous dinosaurs, such as *T. rex*.

Like many early dinosaurs, *Eoraptor* had five-fingered hands.

Turn and learn

Pack hunters: pp. 26–27

"Dawn thief"

Herrera's dinosaur

Find an unknown dinosaur, and it may be named after you. That's what happened to Victorino Herrera after he found fragments of a dinosaur fossil in 1958.

Victorino Herrera's dinosaur was named *Herrerasaurus*. It was one of the earliest dinosaurs.

The slender legs were muscular.

The longest three fingers had curved claws.

weird or what?

Triassic days were shorter than our days. That's because the Earth spun a little faster in Triassic times. It meant that a Triassic day lasted 22¾ hours rather than 24!

Where did Victorino Herrera find the fragments of *Herrerasaurus*?

Pisanosaurus

What did it eat?

Herrerasaurus probably ate mammal-like reptiles called cynodonts.

Thrinaxodon was a small meat-eater. It may have been hairy.

Cynognathus was a ferocious predator with long, doglike teeth.

Diademodon was a plant-eater that grew to the size of a small cow.

Looking out for something small

In addition to cynodonts, *Herrerasaurus* may have feasted on smaller dinosaurs, such as *Pisanosaurus*. Its small frame would have helped it as a stealthy hunter.

The jaws were well-designed to grip struggling prey.

Head talk

Herrerasaurus had a long pointed head and sharp, saw-edged teeth. Its jaw was double-hinged to help it grip its prey.

A long tail helped to balance the body.

A rare find

A near-complete skeleton of *Herrerasaurus* was found in 1988 near the Andes mountains, South America. It showed the dinosaur to be one of the largest hunters of its time. It was a little longer than a car.

Herrerasaurus

Adult human   *Pisanosaurus*

45

In Argentina, where he lived.

Ghost Ranch

Edwin H. Colbert (left) with members of his team.

A fossil quarry in New Mexico is the site of one of the most incredible dinosaur finds ever. Hundreds of dinosaurs died there.

What was found?

In 1947, Edwin H. Colbert documented the discovery of hundreds of well-preserved *Coelophysis* skeletons at Ghost Ranch, New Mexico. This meat-eating dinosaur was one of Earth's first dinosaurs.

Herd of *Coelophysis*

A look at *Coelophysis*

Coelophysis was about 8 ft (2.4 m) long and weighed about 50 lb (23 kg). Its long slender jaws were lined with sharp teeth—evidence that it ate meat.

How did Ghost Ranch get its name?

Ghost Ranch today

Ghost Ranch is a barren place today, but 220 million years ago it was crisscrossed with rivers prone to flooding.

At Ghost Ranch, *Coelophysis* were discovered under just 2 ft (60 cm) of rock.

Fossilized *Coelophysis* skeletons

Locked in death

The fossilized skeletons were twisted around each other and paleontologists believe that they all died together, their deaths caused by flash floods.

Groups of skeletons were found together.

Large eye sockets suggest *Coelophysis* had keen eyesight.

Were they cannibals?

One *Coelophysis* fossil has a young *Coelophysis* skeleton among its ribs, and it was once thought that adults preyed on younger and weaker members of their own kind. However, this now seems unlikely.

Coelophysis probably walked on its hind limbs and used its forelimbs to catch and hold prey.

The young skeleton can be seen in the animal's stomach area.

47

Jurassic dinosaurs

During the Jurassic, the supercontinent Pangaea began to break apart. The oceans spread over what had been land, and huge areas flooded. The result was widespread shallow seas and milder weather.

Jurassic Earth as it looked between 201 and 145 million years ago.

Brachiosaurus

Sauropods may occasionally have walked through water, but they did not live in water.

Dryosaurus

So what was the Earth like?

Gradually the Earth's habitats became less extreme, encouraging more plant variety and the gradual growth of rain forests. There were fewer areas of desert. Dinosaurs moved to new lands, some roaming huge distances.

Did *T. rex* live during the Jurassic period?

Animal life

The Jurassic saw the appearance of giant plant-eating sauropods, such as *Brachiosaurus*, *Apatosaurus*, and *Diplodocus*. Large meat-eaters also emerged, with killers such as *Allosaurus* and *Dilophosaurus* ready to eat anything they could catch. The dinosaurs ruled the Earth.

Apatosaurus

Diplodocus

Allosaurus

Picture detective

Look through the Jurassic Dinosaurs pages to identify each of the picture clues below.

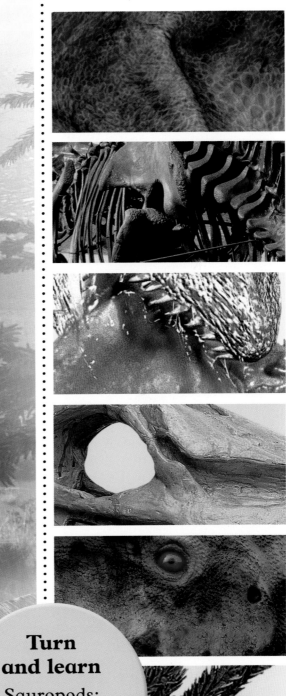

Turn and learn

Sauropods:
pp. 50-55
Allosaurus:
pp. 58-59

49

No, it came later, during the Cretaceous period.

Sauropods

Sauropods were the heaviest, longest, and tallest animals ever to walk on land. They were herbivores, and would have had to graze continually.

Around the world

Sauropods have been found all over the world.

Mamenchisaurus grew to 72 ft (22 m) in length in Jurassic China.

Camarasaurus reached a monstrous 75 ft (23 m) in Jurassic North America.

Barapasaurus grew to lengths of 59 ft (18 m) and roamed Jurassic India.

Vulcanodon was just 21 ft (6.5 m) when it prowled Jurassic Zimbabwe.

Tiny-brained eating machines

Sauropods had tiny heads compared to their bodies. Peg-shaped teeth were used to gather vegetation.

Diplodocus skull

Peg-shaped teeth

Diplodocus's neck and tail made up most of its length.

Look at the size of it!

Imagine a dinosaur that was as long as a tennis court—an adult *Diplodocus* was!

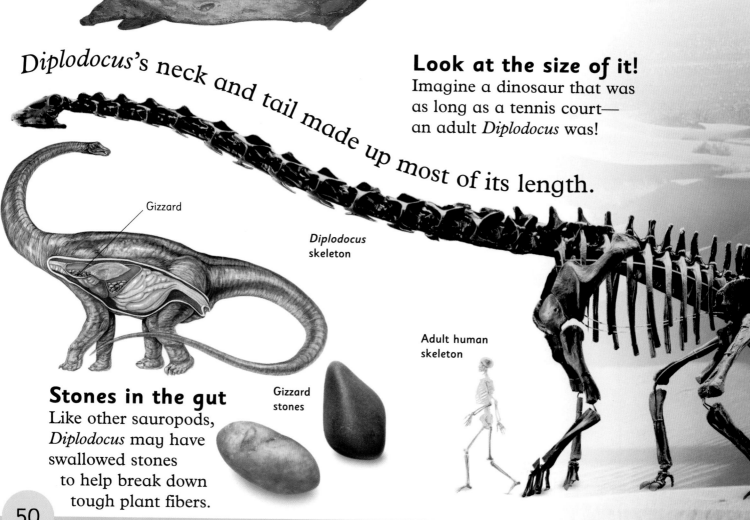

Gizzard

Diplodocus skeleton

Adult human skeleton

Stones in the gut

Like other sauropods, *Diplodocus* may have swallowed stones to help break down tough plant fibers.

Gizzard stones

50

How many neck vertebrae did the *Diplodocus* have?

It's like a giraffe!

Brachiosaurus had longer forelimbs than hind limbs, so its back sloped down to its hindquarters—rather like a giraffe. But *Brachiosaurus* could reach two or three times higher than a giraffe.

Join hands with eight friends and stretch out your arms. That's about the length of *Brachiosaurus*'s neck!

Sauropods had long tails that helped to balance their bodies.

Up high

Brachiosaurus nibbled leaves at the tops of trees. Its long neck may have helped the *Brachiosaurus* to feed where other plant-eaters could not reach.

Sauropods under attack

A sauropod's size was its defense—a full-grown, healthy adult would have been too large to attack. Some were massive. However, the young and sick were vulnerable.

The height of defense

A *Barosaurus* may have reared up to protect its young. Standing on its hind legs, it would have been as tall as a four-story building—about 50 ft (15 m).

Replica neck bones of a *Barosaurus* are carried to an exhibition in New York City.

Barosaurus

How long could a sauropod live?

Diplodocus

Barosaurus   **Apatosaurus**   ♂ Adult human

A Diplodocus was about 108 ft (33 m) long.

Diplodocus used its peg-shaped teeth to strip leaves from tall conifer trees.

A whip in the tail
A tail can make a good whip, and scientists believe that *Apatosaurus* (originally called *Brontosaurus*) may have whipped its tail at predators. This could have resulted in a nasty injury.

On the attack
There was no shortage of Jurassic meat-eating dinosaurs.

Ceratosaurus lived on tree-covered plains and ate dinosaurs and reptiles.

Saurophaganax is thought by scientists to be a type of *Allosaurus*.

Torvosaurus had a bulky body and was the largest carnivore of its time.

Look up!
Diplodocus is the longest dinosaur ever found. It weighed as much as six elephants.

Allosaurus

Allosaurus bit into its prey, then pulled its head up, tearing away flesh.

weird or what?
Diplodocus eggs have been found in lines—not in nests. Scientists believe the animals may have laid their eggs while they walked along!

Probably about 80 years.

Cetiosaurus

Meet an ancient giant—
the *Cetiosaurus*. On a diet
of ferns and trees, it grew
to huge proportions. Its thigh
bone alone was more than
6 ft (1.8 m)—the length
of a full-grown man!

We are family!

Like all dinosaurs,
Cetiosaurus belongs to
a family. It is a part
of the cetiosauridae
family, whose members
lived all over the world.
Here's one of its
Chinese cousins,
Shunosaurus.

Shunosaurus

It's not a whale!

Cetiosaurus was the first sauropod to
be found and one of the first dinosaurs
to be named. Originally, it was believed
to be related to the whale because its
backbones, or vertebrae, were similar
to those of a whale.

Cetiosaurus vertebra

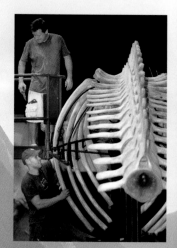

Whale vertebrae

So just how big?

Although only medium-sized for a sauropod,
Cetiosaurus was an impressive 53 ft (16 m) long.
Large herds lived by an ancient sea in the area
we now call England.

What does the name *Cetiosaurus* mean?

What about elsewhere?

The huge *Rhoetosaurus* was one of Australia's largest Jurassic dinosaurs. Because of its great weight, it probably walked slowly and did not run.

Large feet spread *Rhoetosaurus's* weight over a wide area.

Hungry predators

A number of hungry Jurassic meat-eaters might have killed and eaten *Cetiosaurus*.

Megalosaurus was 26 ft (8 m) long. It had curved teeth and long, sharp claws.

Eustreptospondylus was 16–22 ft (5–6.5 m) tall. It was a lightly built hunter.

Poekilopleuron was 30 ft (9 m) long with knifelike teeth that sliced into its prey.

Turn and learn

Living in herds: pp. 30-31

"Whalelike lizard."

We ate plants, too!

The bulky sauropods weren't the only herbivorous dinosaurs in the Jurassic world. A variety of small, plant-eating dinosaurs were also competing for food.

Tough stalks? No problem!

Unlike the sauropods, many smaller plant-eaters had horny, toothless beaks and ridged cheek teeth. They used these to strip tough leaves from woody stems.

Other herbivores

Here are some more Jurassic plant-eaters that you may not know.

Heterodontosaurus, the "different-toothed lizard," had three kinds of teeth.

Lufengosaurus had a horse-sized body. It was a sturdily built prosauropod.

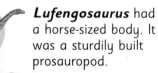

Lesothosaurus had a slim body that was only the size of a small goat.

Were two legs best?

These small plant-eaters had the ability to walk on two legs. This made them far more agile than the bulky sauropods.

How do we know so much about the plants the dinosaurs ate?

Camptosaurus skeleton

Camptosaurus

I'm a survivor
This dinosaur spans two periods—it survived from the late Triassic into the early Cretaceous in North America and England.

Cycads resembled palms we see today, but they didn't produce flowers.

Scutellosaurus

The bony spikes would have made *Scutellosaurus* a lot heavier than other similar-sized dinosaurs.

Don't eat me!
Aside from good agility, some plant-eaters had extra protection. *Scutellosaurus* was covered with more than 300 little bony spikes on its back, sides, and tail.

Conifer trees were plentiful long before the dinosaurs came along.

Horsetails grew taller than many trees in the Mesozoic Era.

Dryosaurus

Ferns were around long before the appearance of the dinosaurs.

Parrot face
Dryosaurus had a parrotlike beak, which it used to crop plants that it then crushed up with its leaf-shaped teeth. It probably lived in herds in East Africa and North America.

Dryosaurus was perfectly built to run away from danger—fast!

Turn and learn
What dinosaurs saw: **pp. 10-11** *Lesothosaurus:* **p. 41**

57

We know because there are lots of fossilized plants.

Killers on the loose

Huge and powerful meat-eaters roamed during the Jurassic. Scientists aren't sure if they hunted singly or in packs, but they would have been formidable predators even when hunting alone.

Turn and learn
Triassic meat-eaters:
pp. 42–45
Cretaceous meat-eater:
pp. 76–77

Allosaurus
This meat-eater used its good hearing and sense of smell to find a victim. It may have hidden in bushes and jumped out on prey that walked by.

Where was the first almost-complete *Allosaurus* found?

Bony crest

What an odd head!
Dilophosaurus, a large two-legged predator, had a semicircular bony crest on either side of its skull. These may have helped cool the dinosaur or been used as part of a mating display.

Dilophosaurus prowled long before *Allosaurus* came on the scene.

What a big head!
Allosaurus's head was 3 ft (1 m) long. Special joints allowed the animal to open its jaws extra wide, exposing about 70 teeth, some 4 in (10 cm) long.

A savage hand
Allosaurus's muscled forearms ended in three-digit, grasping hands. They were equipped with savage, hooked claws.

Allosaurus hand fossil

China's killers

Yangchuanosaurus is hunting. This large meat-eater has spotted a weak *Mamenchisaurus*, a supersized plant-eater, and is waiting for its chance to attack.

What's that dinosaur?

Yangchuanosaurus was a large meat-eater that hunted in Jurassic China. With a head the size of an armchair, it would have been a frightening sight.

Deadly dinosaurs

During the Jurassic, dinosaur numbers continued to grow. Here are more meat-eaters from China.

Dilophosaurus, from the early Jurassic, was found in China and the US.

Monolophosaurus, one of the first giant meat-eaters, was from the mid-Jurassic.

Szechuanosaurus, from the late Jurassic, looked like a small *Allosaurus*.

As with all dinosaurs, we can only guess at this one's skin color and patterning.

Yangchuanosaurus

Mamenchisaurus's long tail helped to balance its neck (a bit like a seesaw balances).

What did *Mamenchisaurus* eat?

There's the end

Mamenchisaurus's long neck was supported by 19 vertebrae. That's the highest number of neck bones of any known dinosaur. The bones were hollow; otherwise the neck would have been too heavy to lift.

Mamenchisaurus's head was less than 2 ft (60 cm) long.

Mamenchisaurus

Famed for its neck

Mamenchisaurus had an absurdly long neck. In fact, its neck was more than half the length of the whole animal and it is currently known as the longest-necked animal ever. Its head, in comparison, was tiny.

It's doubtful that *Mamenchisaurus* could bend its neck very much.

weird or what?

The Moon was a little closer to Earth in Triassic and Jurassic times, making it appear larger in the sky. It would have reflected more of the Sun's light, and so have appeared brighter.

Plants including conifers, seed ferns, club mosses, and horsetails.

Little and large

Although they would not have met, *Compsognathus* and *Ceratosaurus* both lived during the Jurassic—one on warm islands and one on floodplains.

Fossil evidence

Compsognathus was found in 1861, but not at first recognized as a dinosaur as it was thought to be too small. One fossil was found with its last meal inside it—a lizard.

Tiny bones were found in the stomach area.

Fossilized *Compsognathus*

Compsognathus was named after its jaw. The name means "pretty jaw."

Compsognathus was about the size of a chicken.

Living quarters

Compsognathus lived on a group of islands that were where Europe is now. It was a fierce (though small) predator.

What did *Compsognathus* eat?
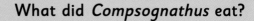

Ceratosaurs

Ceratosaurus belongs to a family of dinosaurs called ceratosaurs. Other members may include:

Dilophosaurus was almost 20 ft (6 m) long and weighed as much as a horse.

Segisaurus was a small ceratosaur, at just 3 ft (1 m) long.

Coelophysis was about 6 ft (1.8 m) long and looked like a long-legged bird.

Ceratosaurus had bony knobs and ridges on its head, spine, and at the end of its tail.

Flexible tail

Ceratosaurus

Ceratosaurus was 15–20 ft (4.5–6 m) long. It was a powerful meat-eating dinosaur with a short horn on its head.

Ceratosaurus means "horned lizard."

Turn and learn

Fossils:
pp. 100-101

Adult human

Compsognathus

Ceratosaurus

This dinosaur had a fourth toe.

63

Small animals such as lizards and Jurassic birds.

A national monument

From 1909 to 1924, scientists removed 330 tons (300 metric tons) of late Jurassic dinosaur bones from a quarry in Utah. The importance of the find was recognized by the creation of the Dinosaur National Monument there in 1915.

Bones in the wall
The Dinosaur National Monument has a visitor's center built around a wall that contains more than 1,500 dinosaur fossils.

A different landscape
In dinosaur times, the area where the fossils were found was a watering hole. That's why so many creatures gathered there.

How long do you think it took Earl Douglass to remove the *Apatosaurus* skeleton he found?

Plant-eaters

Three-quarters of the bones found at the monument belong to sauropods, such as *Apatosaurus*, *Camarasaurus*, and *Diplodocus*.

Apatosaurus lived about 150 million years ago.

Earl the explorer

We know about the Utah quarry thanks to a man named Earl Douglass, who was hunting for dinosaur fossils in the area in 1909. His first discovery was an *Apatosaurus*. That was just the beginning!

Apatosaurus

Meat-eaters

Three types of meat-eaters were found at the Dinosaur National Monument.

Ceratosaurus had a bony horn on its nose. It was a big dinosaur.

Ornitholestes probably preyed on small lizards.

Allosaurus was a large meat-eater. Learn more on page 59.

Apatosaurus had a thick, muscular neck.

The bony plates would have made this dinosaur appear much bigger than it actually was.

Stegosaurus

I recognize that one!

A complete *Stegosaurus* skeleton was found at the monument. This was a small-headed plant-eater that has become famous for its bony plates.

Broad hind foot with three short toes.

65

It took him six years.

Cretaceous dinosaurs

Cretaceous Earth as it looked between 145 and 66 million years ago.

At this time, Earth's continents had separated and were beginning to drift apart. On each one, dinosaurs developed in different ways, so the number of different types of dinosaurs increased significantly.

Corythosaurus

So what was Earth like?

The beginning of the Cretaceous period saw similar temperatures to those in the Jurassic, but over the next million years or so, temperatures began to cool. The Earth we know was beginning to emerge.

Triceratops

What is the oldest flowering plant found so far called and where was its fossil found?

Animal life

The Cretaceous period saw a huge variety of dinosaurs, from plant-eaters such as *Corythosaurus* and *Triceratops* to meat-eaters such as *Troodon* and *T. rex*. They were the last big dinosaurs to live on Earth, and they flourished.

T. rex

Troodon

Picture detective

Look through the Cretaceous Dinosaurs pages to identify each of the picture clues below.

Turn and learn

Troodon:
pp. 82-83
Horned dinosaurs:
pp. 72-73

It is called *Archaeofructus sinensis*. Its 125-million-year-old-fossil was found in China.

Dinosaur Provincial Park

Today, Dinosaur Provincial Park in Alberta, Canada, is rocky and fairly bare. Seventy-five million years ago, it was a subtropical paradise, based around the marshy mouth of a river. It was also the site of an incredible amount of dinosaur activity.

Dinosaur Provincial Park has proved a treasure trove for dinosaur fossils since the first find in 1910.

Fabulous fossilization

Many of the Park's dinosaur skeletons have been well-preserved because of the original marshy ground; just look at this *Corythosaurus*, a hadrosaur.

Fossilized *Corythosaurus* skeleton

What's been found?

Thirty-five species of late Cretaceous dinosaurs have been found at the Park, and a total of 300 skeletons removed. Most common were hadrosaurs.

Corythosaurus

It's a tank!

Euoplocephalus, a plant-eater, was well protected from a possible attack.

Euoplocephalus

What was a key feature of ankylosaurs?

Turtle fossil

What else was found?

In addition to dinosaurs, scientists have found the fossilized skeletons of many other Cretaceous creatures at the Park. These include lots of fish, crocodiles, pterosaurs, birds, mammals, and turtles.

He'll eat me!

Albertosaurus was the Park's largest predator. It would have had plenty of hadrosaurs to feed on.

Armored tanks

Three kinds of ankylosaur dinosaurs have been found at Provincial Park.

Panoplosaurus had long shoulder spikes, as well as bony plates on its back.

Edmontonia was covered with rows of bony plates and spikes.

Euoplocephalus used a hefty lump of bone on its tail for protection.

Albertosaurus looked a little like *T. rex*. In fact, it was related to *T. rex* but it appeared first.

Broad diet

Pachycephalosaurus (see p. 20) had different types of teeth, which may mean that it ate different types of food, such as plants, nuts, and fruit.

More than 170 different types of plant grew in the area.

Pachycephalosaurus

Turn and learn

Ankylosaurs: **pp. 74-75** Hadrosaurs: **pp. 70-71**

69

Most ankylosaurs were heavily armored.

Cretaceous cows

Hadrosaurs, which grazed on all fours, were basically the cows of the Cretaceous. They would have been a familiar sight in North America.

All sorts of crests
Those striking crests came in all kinds of different shapes.

Corythosaurus had a platelike crest.

***Tsintaosaurus*'s** crest may have been covered in brightly colored skin.

Lambeosaurus had a helmetlike crest.

Hadrosaurs had stiff tails. It is unlikely these were swung from side to side.

Male hadrosaurs probably had larger crests than the females.

Parasaurolophus

What a sight!
Hadrosaurs are known for having some of the strangest heads of all dinosaurs; many of them had a crest.

Turn and learn
Another hadrosaur, *Maiasaura*: **pp. 24–25**

Can you think of any crested animals today?

A hadrosaur had more than 1,000 teeth (although not all were in use at the same time).

What did they eat?

One hadrosaur fossil contained the remains of its last meal—bark, pinecones, conifer needles, and branches. Such tough plant matter is particularly hard to digest.

Did they have teeth?

The beaked jaws contained tightly packed rows of teeth to grind vegetation.

Fossilized hadrosaur teeth

Corythosaurus

Chew and move on

A hadrosaur such as *Corythosaurus* would have roamed in huge herds, grazing on leaves, pine needles, and ferns.

A number of lizards and birds have crests.

Horns and frills

Built like a rhinoceros, *Triceratops* is one of the best-known of all dinosaurs. It belongs to a group known as the "horned face" dinosaurs, or ceratopsians.

That's one hefty plant-eater!

In the big league
Triceratops was one of the largest of all the horned faces, reaching about 33 ft (10 m) in length when fully grown.

What does the name *Triceratops* mean?

Other ceratopsians

There were a number of different dinosaurs with horns and frills.

Protoceratops had a head frill but lacked a horn.

Styracosaurus, or "spiked lizard," had a fancy, horned frill.

Pentaceratops had an enormous neck frill and three long horns.

Sheep of the Gobi

Protoceratops roamed the Gobi Desert in Asia like sheep roam today. In fact, they were about the size of sheep.

Like all the horned-face dinosaurs, *Protoceratops* had a parrotlike beak.

Fully developed skull

That's not a fighter

Protoceratops lacked any protection. Its small size would have made it the ideal prey for a number of meat-eaters.

Here you can see the growth of a *Protoceratops* skull, from baby to a full-grown adult.

A big graveyard

The Gobi Desert is littered with the remains of *Protoceratops*, and they show all stages of growth.

Hatchling's skull

73

Ankylosaurus skull

Armored tanks

The ankylosaurs were the armored tanks of the dinosaur world. These four-legged dinosaurs had their own form of protection because they were covered in thick bony plates and spikes.

Armored head

Ankylosaurs were protected from head to tail. Just look at the solid appearance of these fossilized skulls.

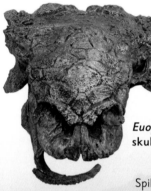

Euoplocephalus skull

Armored giant

At one time, *Euoplocephalus* was a common ankylosaur on the plains of North America. This creature was well protected from predators by the fused bony plates covering its neck and back.

Euoplocephalus

Spikes and studs added extra protection.

Broad beak helped in cropping ferns and low-growing plants.

74

Were ankylosaurs meat-eaters or plant-eaters?

Ankylosaurs

Ankylosaurs can be separated into groups depending on their appearance. Below are three main groups.

Ankylosaurids, such as *Ankylosaurus*, had bony clubs on their tails.

Nodosaurids, such as *Edmontonia*, had rows of spikes on their bodies.

Polacanthids, such as *Gastonia*, had spiked bodies and tails.

Impressions in rock show that *Saltasaurus* had bony studs.

Saltasaurus

Armored sauropods, too!

The ankylosaurs were not the only Cretaceous dinosaurs to have armor. Some sauropods did, too. Just look at this studded *Saltasaurus*.

Ankylosaurus tail club

Clubbed tail

Some ankylosaurs had a tail club made of fused bone that they would swing at attackers. The weighty club would have been a formidable weapon.

They were plant-eaters.

T. rex

The mighty *T. rex* roamed North America in the last couple of million years that dinosaurs ruled the planet.

T. rex's eyeballs were the size of a clenched fist.

Titanic teeth

T. rex had awesome curved teeth, each as long as a human hand. Altogether, it had 58 of these pointed weapons.

T. rex preyed on plant-eaters such as *Triceratops*.

T. rex walked on its powerful hind limbs.

When teeth broke, new ones grew to replace them.

Was it a killer?

We don't really know if *T. rex* was a hunter or a scavenger. It may have attacked and killed, or it may have picked at dead or dying dinosaurs. It may have done both.

T. rex is short for *Tyrannosaurus rex*. What does it mean?

Lighten up

With its massive skull that was 5 ft (1.5 m) long, this beast could swallow small dinosaurs whole! Spaces between the skull bones made it lighter.

A *T. rex* had tiny serrations on its teeth. Its bite would have torn into a victim's flesh.

Guanlong was just 3 ft 6 in (1.1 m) tall, but most of that was tail and neck!

My ancestor

One of the oldest members of the tyrannosaur family was recently found in China. *Guanlong* prowled Earth some 100 million years before *T. rex*.

What a whopper!

Meet Sue, the world's largest and most complete *T. rex* skeleton. She was sold to an American museum in 1991 for a jaw-dropping $8 million.

Nose to tail, Sue measures 42 ft (12.8 m).

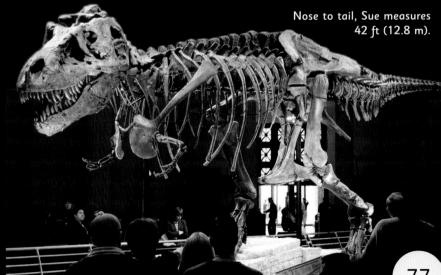

Tyrannosaurus rex means "king of the tyrant lizards."

Big and bold

Giganotosaurus means "giant southern reptile," and this dinosaur was big. In fact, it may have been larger than *T. rex*. However, the two never met, because *Giganotosaurus* was roaming Earth 10 million years before *T. rex*!

It's a new find!
Giganotosaurus bones were first unearthed in Argentina in the early 1990s, but no complete skeleton has ever been found.

Giganotosaurus would have had a keen sense of smell and excellent eyesight.

weird or what?
It's difficult to imagine just how big and heavy a full-grown *Giganotosaurus* really was. It's thought to have been as heavy as about 125 adult humans. That's a lot of people!

Where did *Giganotosaurus* live?

Let's get it!

A huge sauropod, *Argentinosaurus* lived alongside *Giganotosaurus*. It's thought that this monster may have reached 140 ft (43 m) in length. So one *Giganotosaurus*, which was 45 ft (13.5 m) long, couldn't have brought it down, but these predators may have hunted in packs.

Argentinosaurus

Turn and learn

Sauropods:
pp. 50-53
T. rex:
pp. 76-77

Awesome arms

Giganotosaurus had larger and more powerful forearms than *T. rex*, and they were three-fingered. The fingers would have been used to grasp prey and food.

That's some tooth!

Giganotosaurus had large, serrated teeth that helped in stabbing and gripping prey, as well as slashing through the meat. The largest teeth were about 8 in (20 cm) long.

In the warm swamps of Cretaceous Argentina.

Spinosaurus

If there is a contender for the dinosaur that most resembled a dragon, then surely this is it. With its tall "sail" and long, narrow jaws, *Spinosaurus* would have been a frightening sight.

What's that on its back?
Spinosaurus had an impressive skin "sail" that ran the length of its back. The sail was supported by a number of bones measuring up to 6 ft (1.8 m).

African elephant

What was it for?
The sail bones were covered with a fine mesh of tiny veins, just like an elephant's ears. An elephant cools itself by flapping its ears. The sail may have helped to cool the *Spinosaurus*.

Where and when were the first fossils of *Spinosaurus* discovered?

Did it look like that?

No one actually knows what color any particular dinosaur was. *Spinosaurus* could have been a dull shade, or it may have been more brightly decorated.

Spinosaurus was closely related to *Baryonyx* (see p. 88).

Spinosaurus may have been as colorful and patterned as some of the snakes we see today.

Spinosaurus had crocodile-like teeth and preyed on fish by wading into the water.

We are family

There was a great variety of size within dinosaur groups. *Spinosaurus*, which was bigger than *T. rex*, belonged to a group of dinosaurs called the spinosaurs. One of *Spinosaurus*'s smallest relatives was a South American dinosaur called *Irritator*.

weird or what?

Irritator got its strange name after an irritating episode when its fossilized remains were altered by its finder in an attempt to make it more valuable.

Fossil remains of *Irritator* have been found in Brazil.

It was found in Egypt, in 1912.

A bright spark?

Troodon is believed to have been the most intelligent of the dinosaurs, given the size of its brain in relation to its body.

Night hunter?

Scientists believe *Troodon* had good vision. It may even have had vertical pupils (just like a cat's) that would have helped it to hunt at night.

Models of *Troodon*

Turn and learn

Dinosaur eggs and nests: **pp. 22-23**

Troodon's long slender limbs would have made it extremely agile.

A large sickle-shaped claw on *Troodon*'s second toe was used to tear and slash.

What might *Troodon* have hunted?

Let's look at a tooth

"*Troodon*" means "wounding tooth."
The small teeth were serrated
and hooked backward to
help *Troodon* grip
struggling prey.

Troodon
tooth

A *Troodon* had about
120 teeth in its mouth.
A human child has 20.

Troodon was
probably feathered.

Grab and go

Troodon had
three-fingered
hands tipped
with sharp
claws that
would have
been ideal for
grabbing and
then holding
onto its prey.

My nest!

There is evidence that *Troodon*
lived in large colonies, caring for
their young. Suspected *Troodon*
nests found in Montana were
6 ft (1.8 m) wide and contained
up to 24 eggs.

Probably baby dinosaurs, small mammals, snakes, lizards, and birds.

Meet the raptors

Velociraptor

The narrow jaws contained about 80 sharp teeth.

The feathers would have been used for warmth, not flight.

Aggressive and speedy, *Velociraptor* was a formidable predator in late Cretaceous Asia. Although small, it was armed with razor-sharp teeth and terrifying daggerlike claws.

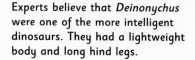

Bambiraptor

A feathered dinosaur?

Some dinosaur fossils have been found with traces of a featherlike covering, and it's thought that *Velociraptor* may have had feathers, though no *Velociraptor* fossil has been found with them.

Experts believe that *Deinonychus* were one of the more intelligent dinosaurs. They had a lightweight body and long hind legs.

The killer claw

Deinonychus had a vicious killer claw on each of its hind legs. It held the claw off the ground, and slashed its victims with it.

Deinonychus foot fossil

84

What does the name *Velociraptor* mean?

This skeleton has been mounted to show *Deinonychus* leaping toward a victim, claws ready.

Deinonychus skeleton

Velociraptor and *Deinonychus* belong to a group called the dromaeosaurids. Scientists believe these killing machines were related to the birds alive today.

Jump and grab
Velociraptor and its relations, such as the larger *Deinonychus*, may have hunted in packs and jumped onto the back of their prey, all four limbs extended.

Deinonychus means "terrible claw."

"Speedy thief." Scientists believe it may have reached 40 mph (65 kph).

A pot-bellied dinosaur!

Is this the most bizarre of all the dinosaurs?
Therizinosaurus certainly had the longest
known arms, tipped with fingers that had
claws up to 2 ft (60 cm) long.

A strange cousin

An odd-looking
dinosaur from
the same family
as *Therizinosaurus*
was *Beipiaosaurus*.
Evidence shows that
its arms and legs
were covered with
downy feathers.

Leatherback turtle

Are they flippers?

Therizinosaurus had such strange-
looking arms that when its claws
were first found, they were believed
to belong to a giant turtle.

Do you think *Therizinosaurus* was a meat-eater or a plant-eater?

Puzzle time

Scientists have had to piece together an idea of what the *Therizinosaurus* looked like because very little of it has been found (in fact, only the arms!). Its appearance in books today is based upon finds of other members of the therizinosaur family. Ideas may change.

Recent studies have found that *Therizinosaurus* may have had fine feathers. We don't know for certain.

A plant-eater. It looked threatening, but it had a toothless beak.

Fish dinner

Ninety million years ago, a dinosaur stands watching silently by a large lake. Suddenly, claws flash in the sunlight, and a fish the length of your leg, a *Lepidotes*, is caught. Meet the fishing dinosaur, *Baryonyx*!

Fossilized *Lepidotes*

Toadstones

Fishy tale
Lepidotes was a Mesozoic fish that was found in lakes and shallow seas. *Lepidotes* teeth are a common fossil find in Southern England, where they are known as toadstones.

Did it really eat fish?
Baryonyx's crocodile-like jaws were perfect for grabbing fish, but we also know it ate fish because fossilized fish scales and bones were found with this dinosaur's fossil.

Baryonyx

How did toadstones get their name?

Look at that claw!

Baryonyx's name means "heavy claw." It was given this name because of its huge thumb claws. The long, curved claws were ideal for stabbing and snatching fish from the water.

Baryonyx's claw measures 12 in (30 cm) along the outside edge.

I found it first

The first fossilized claw of *Baryonyx* was found in England in the early 1980s by an amateur fossil collector named William Walker.

The jaw contains 96 pointed teeth.

Hidden secrets

After the claw was found, about 60 percent of the dinosaur was gradually uncovered in surrounding rocks, including this near-perfect skull.

Fossilized *Baryonyx* skull

89

Hundreds of years ago, people thought they came from the heads of living toads!

Other forms of life

When dinosaurs were around, there were other prehistoric creatures also, some of which swam in the sea or flew. So what other creatures coexisted with the dinosaurs?

Life, but not as we know it

Throughout the Mesozoic Era, dinosaurs existed alongside other groups of animals that lived on land and in the oceans, such as mammals and other reptiles. Some of these reptiles could fly.

Would dinosaurs have eaten pterosaurs?

Pterosaurs existed from the late Triassic period to the end of the Cretaceous period.

Plesiosaurs were most common during the Jurassic period.

Turn and learn
Plesiosaurs:
pp. 92-93
Pterosaurs:
pp. 94-95

Yes, if they managed to catch them!

Picture detective

Look through the Other Forms of Life pages to identify each of the picture clues below.

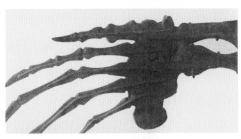

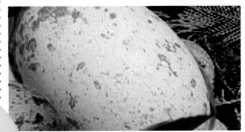

Monsters of the deep

Ichthyosaurus

There may have been no marine dinosaurs, but an astonishing variety of toothed giant reptiles ruled the seas while the dinosaurs ruled the land.

Ichthyosaurs had large eyes.

Elasmosaurus was air-breathing, and just like whales today, it had to come to the surface to breathe.

Its neck was as long as its body.

Swim away...

An *Ichthyosaurus* moved swiftly to keep from being eaten. The swimming ichthyosaurs, including *Ichthyosaurus* itself, were perfectly suited for chasing fast-moving prey, such as squid. They were, however, vulnerable to attack from larger marine reptiles.

... from danger!

Watch out! A *Liopleurodon* is attacking the ichthyosaurs from below. Perhaps the largest sea-based predator of all time, *Liopleurodon* was a short-necked plesiosaur.

What did *Liopleurodon* eat?

Elasmosaurus

What's that?

Elasmosaurus was also a plesiosaur, but it was long-necked. Its four paddle-shaped limbs propelled it easily through the water. It grew up to 46 ft (14 m) in length.

I recognize that!

Many Mesozoic occupants of the Earth's seas would have been familiar to us.

Jellyfish have been around for about 400 million years.

Corals are fragile animals, but they have managed to survive since the dinosaurs.

The **great white shark**'s ancestors date back to the Cretaceous period.

Squid were on the menu for ichthyosaurs, shown by fossil evidence.

Snails are also present in fossil form, showing they too are great survivors.

The remains of the largest-known specimen of *Liopleurodon* indicate a maximum length of about 33 ft (10 m).

Liopleurodon

The daggerlike teeth were twice as long as those of *T. rex*.

weird or what?

Some people think the "monster" in Loch Ness, a Scottish Lake, is a plesiosaur that was trapped there when the sea receded millions of years ago!

Anything it could catch, including pterosaurs that flew too close to the water's surface.

Monsters of the air

No dinosaur flew, but they had relatives that did—the pterosaurs, or flying reptiles. Some were tiny, but others had the wingspan of a small airplane.

Who came first?
Early pterosaurs had long tails and narrow wings. They were fairly small—*Dimorphodon* and *Rhamphorhynchus* were about 3 ft (1 m) in length.

The tail was used to control the direction of flight.

Rhamphorhynchus

Dimorphodon

Dimorphodon had a large, puffinlike head, with a toothed beak.

What did they eat?
Lots of pterosaur fossils have been found in coastal areas, suggesting they swooped low over the sea, picking off fish. They probably also caught insects.

Were pterosaurs a type of bird?

Pterodactylus

Look at mine!
Many Cretaceous pterosaurs had crests. They may have been used to attract mates.

Tropeognathus had a large crest at the end of its upper jaw.

Anhanguera had a crest on its upper and lower jaw.

Pteranodon had a long, backward-pointing crest.

Dsungaripterus had two crests on the top of its head.

Did they have fur?
The pterosaurs probably had fur, like modern-day bats. They also had large eyes, giving them excellent vision.

Tropeognathus

It's the size of a plane!
A male *Tropeognathus* may have had a wingspan of 20 ft (6 m), although it weighed less than a seven-year-old child.

Each wing was made of skin that grew between the leg and an extra-long bone of the fourth finger.

Quetzalcoatlus

Who was the biggest?
By the Cretaceous period, pterosaurs had grown bigger. Possibly the largest flying reptile of all was found in Texas in the 1930s. *Quetzalcoatlus* had a wingspan of 39–46 ft (12–14 m).

No. Pterosaurs were winged reptiles and were not related to birds.

Were there mammals?

Mammals began to appear in the late Cretaceous period, but they were small and were dominated by the success of the dinosaurs. They were to become incredibly successful eventually, but it took millions of years.

Are they really that small?

Primitive mammals began to appear in the late Triassic, some 220 million years ago, and they were tiny. Just look at the mammal timeline shown below with its comparison to the size of an adult human's hand. These mammals were probably nocturnal, hiding in leaf litter and hunting for insects and maybe even dinosaur eggs.

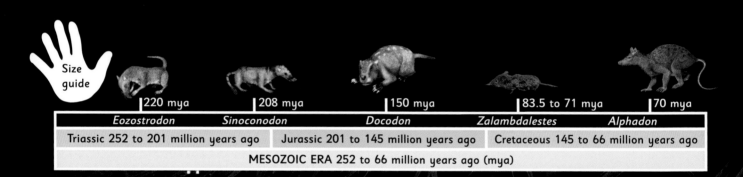

Size guide	220 mya	208 mya	150 mya	83.5 to 71 mya	70 mya
	Eozostrodon	Sinoconodon	Docodon	Zalambdalestes	Alphadon
	Triassic 252 to 201 million years ago		Jurassic 201 to 145 million years ago	Cretaceous 145 to 66 million years ago	
	MESOZOIC ERA 252 to 66 million years ago (mya)				

Early mammals probably raided dinosaur eggs if they had the chance.

Why would early mammals have been nocturnal?

When did mammals get big?

The first large predatory mammals, the creodonts, didn't emerge until Paleocene times (the period of time after the extinction of the dinosaurs).

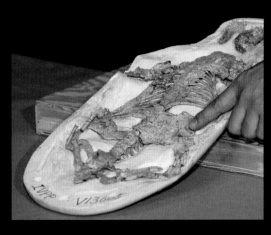

Did mammals eat dinosaurs?

Paleontologists recently found a fossilized *Repenomamus*, a badger-sized beast. That's enormous for a Mesozoic mammal! It even had the remains of baby dinosaurs in its gut.

Look-alike

Another early mammal was the platypus-like *Steropodon*. Like the platypus today, this mammal probably laid eggs.

Early mammals, such as *Docodon*, walked on all fours, had long tails, and long bodies and snouts.

weird or what?
Dinosaurs were amazingly successful—they ruled the Earth for 180 million years. Humans emerged some 200,000 years ago. That's a tiny amount of geological time.

This would have allowed them to keep from being eaten by reptiles and dinosaurs.

Size matters

The creatures that lived during the Mesozoic Era varied dramatically in size—some were tiny, but others grew to enormous proportions.

Mononykus skull

Is that its skull?
Some dinosaurs were really small. This little dinosaur's skull is shown life-sized.

That's not so big...
Ichthyosaurs varied in size. Some were as small as your arm, while many were the size of a dolphin.

Ichthyosaurs are one of the best-known of all Mesozoic creatures.

... but that's a giant!
However, in Triassic times, ichthyosaurs reached massive proportions.

The largest ichthyosaur was 75 ft (23 m) in length.

It may look like an enormous fish, but the ichthyosaur was actually a sea-dwelling reptile.

Was the largest ichthyosaur longer than a blue whale?

Archelon fossil

A number of fossilized *Archelon* skeletons have been found that are missing one flipper.

It's a tiny opossum

Alphadon was one of the first marsupials (animals that carry their young in pouches). Kangaroos are also marsupials— but *Alphadon* was tiny.

Is that a turtle?

Archelon was a turtle, but it was three times the size of the largest turtle today. Full-grown adults had shells that were 13 ft (4 m) long.

Alphadon

It lived 210 million years ago.

Ichthyosaurs may have had reddish-brown skin.

Turn and learn
Ichthyosaurs: p. 92

99

No. They were big, but blue whales reach 100 ft (30 m) in length.

Fossils

Fossils have been found all over the world, but they are not easy to recognize and have often been discovered by accident, perhaps following construction work.

The right conditions?

Lots of fossils have been found, but for every fossilized dinosaur, hundreds and thousands died, decayed, and left no trace.

"Fossil" comes from a Latin word that means "dug up."

Fossils are encased in rock that has to be carefully removed.

This fossil, known as Sue, is the largest, most complete *T. rex* fossil ever found. It was named after Sue Hendrickson, a paleontologist who discovered it.

Name one difference between fossilization and mummification.

What kind of fossil is that?

There are different types of fossils. Classification depends on how they were created.

Total preservation

This is when the whole animal is preserved, such as an insect in amber.

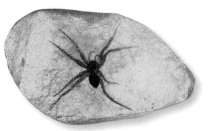

Semi-preservation

This results when just the hard parts of an object are preserved unaltered.

Petrified

Wood is sometimes petrified. It means the hard parts are preserved, but are chemically altered.

Natural mold

This occurs when the animal or plant decays away, leaving a hole in the rock. The paleontologist fills this with latex rubber.

Natural cast

This forms as a mold, but the hole is filled by natural substances. For example, a fossil may be cast in a stone called flint.

Trace fossils

These are fossils that show where an animal has been, such as footprints, nests, or coprolites (animal dung).

Picture detective

Look through the Fossils pages to identify each of the picture clues below.

Turn and learn

How a dinosaur may turn into a fossil: pp. 102–103

Fossils are preserved in the Earth's rocks. Mummification is usually done by people.

How was it made?

Fossils may form when animal or plant matter is buried, soon after death, under mud or sand. However, that's just the beginning of a process that takes millions of years.

70 million years ago
A *T. rex* has died and is washed downstream. It rests on layers of soft mud and is rapidly buried.

Five years later
The creature's soft flesh has slowly rotted away, leaving the bones. Over time, these begin to move apart.

50 million years ago
A sea has now spread over the area once occupied by the river. Heavy pressure is slowly turning the sand to sandstone.

What are some of the things that fossilize?

Two million years ago

The passing of millions of years has seen mountain ranges rising above the fossilized *T. rex*, but gradually they are being worn down by extreme weather.

Last year

The area around the fossil is now a desert. Two walkers investigate further when they see the exposed tip of a fossilized bone.

Today

Paleontologists are now hard at work, uncovering the rest of the *T. rex*. The bones will be removed one by one. The skeleton may end up in a museum.

103

Fossils include bones, teeth, skin impressions, and footprints. Plants also fossilize.

Masses of bones

Certain places are rich in dinosaur fossils. In some areas, dinosaurs may have been drowned in floods; in others, they look like they were caught in traps and many dinosaurs died at about the same time. We can learn a lot from these "dinosaur traps."

A paleontologist investigates one fossil in a wall of fossils formed when lots of dinosaurs drowned in the same place.

What's been found?

Paleontologists studied one dinosaur trap in Utah and discovered more than 10,000 bones. They believe the plant-eaters stopped to drink at a lake and were trapped in deep mud. Predators were trapped when they approached in the hope of an easy meal.

What we can learn

Fossils can tell us how large an animal was, what it ate, and even how it may have died.

An *Allosaurus* tries to attack a *Stegosaurus*. Both will be...

What is a predator?

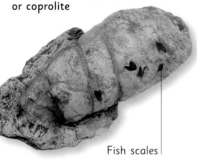

Ichthyosaur dropping, or coprolite

Fish scales

This one ate fish!
Fossilized droppings can tell us what an animal ate. Ichthyosaurs swam in oceans while dinosaurs ruled the land. This fossilized ichthyosaur dropping has clear fish scales.

What we can't learn
Although dinosaur skin impressions exist, we have no way of knowing what color dinosaurs really were.

Dinosaur skin impression

Could *T. rex* have been this colorful?

A complete find?
When paleontologists discover a new dinosaur fossil site, they refer to the bones they find in one of the four ways listed below.

An **articulated** skeleton is a skeleton that is still joined together as it was in life. In rare cases it is almost complete.

An **associated** skeleton is where the bones have broken apart and spread out, but are from the same animal.

Isolated bone is an individual bone that has been separated from the skeleton. It may be a skull or a femur.

Float is what paleontologists call the scraps of bone that are too small to be of use.

After 145 million years, the dinosaur trap is discovered and the fossils exposed.

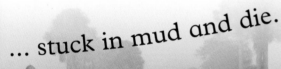

... stuck in mud and die.

A **predator** is an animal that hunts and kills another animal.

Investigating a find

It takes an incredibly long time to excavate and examine a fossil find. Sometimes bones are in sand, but usually they have to be removed from rock, which is chipped away in small sections. All the sand and rock has to be removed.

Paleontologists investigating the site of a new find

Easy does it!

If a skeleton is discovered, most of it may be covered with an immense amount of rock and soil, which has to be cleared away. It's skilled work—no one wants to damage the fossil.

Grid control

It is important that the location and position of the bones are recorded accurately. That's why you'll often see a string grid above a find, so a chart can be mapped.

How might a large fossil be moved once it has its plaster coat?

Don't break it!

At the site, large fossils will be wrapped in bandages and runny plaster of Paris. This will set hard to protect the fossil before it can be moved to a museum, where it can be cleaned and examined.

Paleontologists use a range of equipment.

Paintbrushes are used to remove dust.

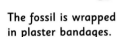

The fossil is wrapped in plaster bandages.

Tools of the trade

You'd find a paleontologist's toolbox pretty ordinary, with hammers, trowels, and a range of paintbrushes.

The work doesn't stop

Back at the museum, the plaster cast is removed and the fossil examined. The work requires patience. It took technicians more than 3,500 hours (about five months) to clean and repair this one *T. rex* skull. Then a cast was made for exhibition.

Paleontologists are dinosaur detectives.

107

Is it real?

Fossil exhibits in museums are sometimes replicas, since these are lighter in weight and the original fossil can then remain in protective storage. So how is the replica made?

It all begins with the bones

First of all, a mold is made of the fossilized bone. It's done by painting liquid rubber onto the fossil's surface.

The liquid rubber will dry to form a flexible mold.

The next job

Once the rubber has solidified, it is covered in liquid plastic strengthened with fiberglass. This supports the rubber and makes it rigid enough to hold the shape when removed from the bones.

Here, a leg bone has been molded in two halves.

108

Here, an *Allosaurus* model is being put together in a museum exhibit.

Ready to show!
The finished bones are now ready to display. A complete skeleton will be assembled in sections before these sections are brought together. The whole operation requires careful planning.

Turn and learn
Assembling the *Barosaurus* for display:
pp. 110-111

Filling up the molds
The shape is then filled with liquid plastic. This will set hard, forming a stiff but lightweight foam. The replica bones need to be light in weight.

Liquid plastic is poured into the mold.

Let's take a look!
Once the plastic has set, the outer molds are carefully removed. Any seams are filed to smooth them, and the foam plastic replica bone (cast) will then be painted to match the original fossil.

The cast is easily removed from its mold.

For making boats and cars, because fiberglass is not only strong but also lightweight.

It's a jigsaw

After fossilized bones have been studied and replicas have been made, a museum may decide to mount a display for people to come and see. It can be a long process.

Stick to the plans
There are a lot of bones in a large dinosaur, and specialists have to be careful to get each bone in the right place.

When finished, this replica would be more than 49 ft (15 m) high.

Ready with the ribs
Sometimes parts of the skeleton's frame are assembled elsewhere and then transported to the museum.

Bring in the machines
Some museums are fortunate enough to have high ceilings, perfect for exhibiting a rearing sauropod. This *Barosaurus* skeleton was so large it needed the help of two cherry-picking machines to position the sections.

How many bones were put together to make the *Barosaurus* skeleton?

Almost done

If a model is enormous, as here, it may need to be supported by metal rods, which have to be welded in place. After all, no one wants a visitor to be hit by a falling bone!

A welder is protected from sparks by a flame-resistant helmet and gloves.

The finished model shows the mother rearing to protect her young from an approaching *Allosaurus*.

111

End of the dinosaurs

The last 10 million years of the Cretaceous period saw a huge variety of dinosaurs. They were flourishing. Yet, the age of dinosaurs was about to come to an end.

Who came up with the theory that dinosaurs became extinct because of a meteorite strike?

Why did they die?

There have been many theories about why the giant dinosaurs died out.

Plague wiped out millions in Europe in the 1300s. Did dinosaurs get sick?

Fire storms, caused by volcanic activity, could have made life harsh.

Meteorites from space may have brought widespread devastation.

Egg predators increased. Did fewer and fewer dinosaur babies survive?

Tsunami created by earthquakes and meteorites destroyed habitats.

As **continents shifted**, climate and vegetation changed. Dinosaurs could not adjust to these changes.

Picture detective

Look through the End of the Dinosaurs pages to identify each of the picture clues below.

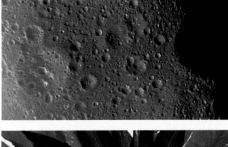

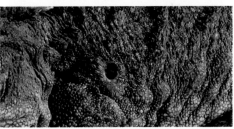

Turn and learn

What happened at the end of the Mesozoic Era:
pp. 114–115

113

What happened?

Sixty-six million years ago, the giant dinosaurs died out, along with the pterosaurs and most marine reptiles. It was a mass extinction, but what caused it? Many believe it was a meteorite.

What changed?
Scientists now believe a massive meteorite hit the Earth, creating a dust cloud of noxious fumes that screened out the Sun and changed the climate.

Who died?
Huge numbers of animals became extinct. Some are listed below.

Pterosaurs had once filled the skies with their airborne acrobatics.

All the different types of **dinosaur** that had evolved died out.

Huge reptiles disappeared from the oceans.

The rock would have hit the Earth's crust with terrific force, sending shock waves around the world.

It was a big one!
In the early 1990s, geologists found the remains of a massive crater in Mexico. It was 112 miles (180 km) wide. They believe it was caused by a meteorite smashing into the Earth 66 million years ago.

How big were the animals that survived the extinction?

Was that all?

The meteorite hit at a time of immense volcanic activity in an area that is now western India. This activity would have sent up clouds of ash and dust that would have blocked the Sun's light—just like the effect of the meteorite hitting the Earth. The extinction may have been a combination of both these events.

The rock that created the Mexican crater was 6 miles (10 km) in diameter.

An exploding volcano sends up clouds of lethal dust.

No land animal heavier than a large dog survived.

Who survived?

It may have been a catastrophic event for the giant dinosaurs, but incredibly, some creatures did survive the great extinction.

Tiny mammals survived the event that killed off *Triceratops*.

They made it!
Among the animals that survived were sharks, jellyfish, fish, scorpions, birds, and insects.

I was there at the end
Fossil records show us that *Triceratops* was one of the last of the big dinosaurs, along with *T. rex*.

An ancient history
Tuataras—curiously spiny reptiles that live on islands off New Zealand—are related to reptiles that were around at the time of the dinosaurs.

Shark

Jellyfish

Tuatara

The tuatara survived the extinction!

Which era came after the Mesozoic Era?

Scaly survivors

Although no large land animals made it, a number of smaller reptiles did outlive the dinosaurs.

 There are now some 2,900 different types of **snake**.

Turtles first appeared about 200 million years ago—before the dinosaurs!

 There are about 4,500 different **lizards**.

Crocodiles largely inhabit freshwater rivers and lakes.

Flying dinosaurs

Modern birds are now known to be living dinosaurs. Birds of prey use their talons to seize food, just like some giant dinosaurs may have.

The Egyptian vulture is a bird of prey.

Turn and learn

Link between birds and dinosaurs: **pp. 118-119**

The Cenozoic Era, which saw the rise of the mammals.

Living dinosaurs

You may think that reptiles are closely related to dinosaurs, but dinosaurs may have more in common with birds!

A hidden link?

The link between dinosaurs and birds is clear when you look at *Caudipteryx*, one of the many feathered dinosaurs.

Caudipteryx, a turkey-sized Cretaceous creature, would not have been able to fly because its wings were too small.

The first bird?

The earliest-known bird is *Archaeopteryx*, which first appeared in the Jurassic period. It had the toothed head, clawed fingers, and long bony tail like that of a dinosaur, but it also had feathers.

Fossilized *Archaeopteryx*

Archaeopteryx means "ancient wing."

118

What size do you think *Archaeopteryx* reached?

Why feathers?

Feathers protect birds from water and from temperature changes, and they may have served the same purpose on the feathered dinosaurs.

Hoatzin are found in parts of South America.

Feathers provide good insulation from cold.

We have claws

Some modern birds have clawed wings. Hoatzin chicks have two tiny claws at the end of each wing. The adults do not use them, but the chicks use them to clamber through trees.

Caudipteryx had clawed hands.

weird or what?

The evidence that birds are directly descended from dinosaurs is getting stronger all the time. This means that dinosaurs are not extinct! They are living all around us, right now.

Caudipteryx was about the size of a turkey.

Pieces of a puzzle

More and more "dino-birds" are being discovered, and each discovery helps our understanding. This model is based on feathered fossils found in China.

Sinosauropteryx

It was small—about the size of a pigeon.

Dinosaur records

The biggest... the smallest... the longest... the tallest... Here are the dinosaur record-breakers!

Fossil of a young *Mussaurus*

As long as a pencil, this young *Mussaurus* lived in the desert lands of Triassic South America. Its name means "mouse lizard."

Smallest dinosaur found: A skeleton of a *Mussaurus* was 8 in (20 cm) long—although it was only a baby.

Longest neck: *Mamenchisaurus's* neck was 46–50 ft (14–15 m) long—about the same as three elephants in a row.

Longest tail: *Diplodocus's* tail was around 43–46 ft (13–14 m) long.

Largest claw: The claws of a *Therizinosaurus* grew to 36 in (91 cm) long—about as long as a man's arm.

Largest egg: *Macroelongatoolithus xixiaensis* eggs found in China were 18 in (46 cm) long.

Largest head: Both *Pentaceratops* and *Torosaurus* had heads more than 10 ft (3 m) long.

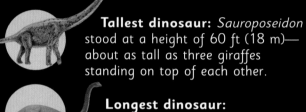
Tallest dinosaur: *Sauroposeidon* stood at a height of 60 ft (18 m)—about as tall as three giraffes standing on top of each other.

Longest dinosaur: *Diplodocus* could reach up to 175 ft (53.3 m).

Biggest meat-eating dinosaur: The 52-ft- (16-m-) long *Spinosaurus* must have been a terrifying predator!

Most teeth: Hadrosaurs, such as *Lambeosaurus*, had more than 1,000 teeth—all for chewing plants!

Smallest adult dinosaur: A full-grown adult *Microraptor* was around 16 in (40 cm) long.

One *Citipati* died on its nest. Some fossil *Citipati* eggs have been found to contain unhatched, fossilized babies.

Will these dinosaur records ever change?

T. rex was among the biggest meat-eaters ever—but it was still smaller than *Spinosaurus*.

Life-size model of *T. rex*

Smallest brain:
Stegosaurus had a brain the size of three ping-pong balls.

Fastest dinosaur:
It is thought that *Dromiceiomimus* reached speeds of 43 mph (70 kph).

Earliest dinosaur:
Eoraptor lived about 228 million years ago, in the Triassic period.

First herd found: The first big hoard of dinosaur skeletons was found in 1878. There were 32 skeletons, all of *Iguanodon*.

The first *Iguanodon* skeletons were found in Belgium by coal miners.

121

True or false?

Can you figure out which of these facts are real, and which ones are made up?

1 Pterosaurs were flying dinosaurs.

4 Caudipteryx, known as a "dino-bird," could fly.

2 Pangaea was a supercontinent in which dinosaurs first lived.

3 Crocodiles are the biggest surviving archosaurs.

6: False—it had more than 1,000 teeth 7: False—it means "five-horned face"

5 Diplodocus had the longest tail among all dinosaurs.

6 A hadrosaur had about 100 teeth.

7 Birds have evolved from lizard-hipped dinosaurs.

8 The name Pentaceratops means "three-horned face."

123

Quiz

Test your knowledge
of dinosaurs with these
quiz questions.

1 Where were the remains of *Iguanodon* first found?

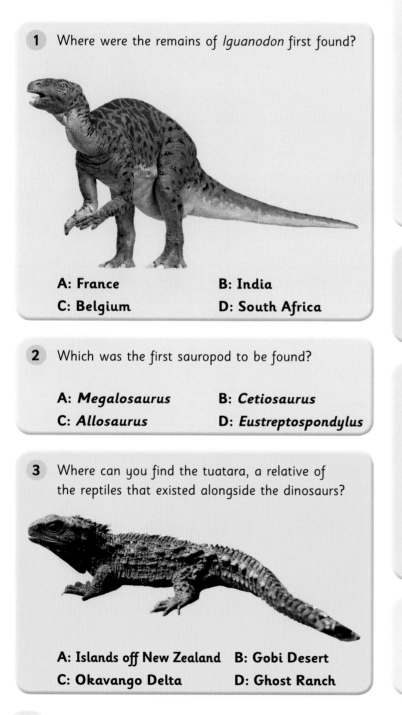

A: France   B: India
C: Belgium   D: South Africa

2 Which was the first sauropod to be found?

A: *Megalosaurus*   B: *Cetiosaurus*
C: *Allosaurus*   D: *Eustreptospondylus*

3 Where can you find the tuatara, a relative of
the reptiles that existed alongside the dinosaurs?

A: Islands off New Zealand   B: Gobi Desert
C: Okavango Delta   D: Ghost Ranch

4 The largest dinosaur egg was laid by...

A: *Macroelongatoolithus*   B: *Citipati*
C: *Therizinosaurus*   D: *Parasaurolophus*

5 What is the nickname of the world's largest and
most complete *T. rex* skeleton?

A: Sara   B: Joan
C: Sue   D: Lucy

6 Which of these was the earliest-known bird?

A: *Caudipteryx*   B: *Sinosauropteryx*
C: *Archaeopteryx*   D: *Quetzalcoatlus*

7 Which dinosaur is also known as a "living tank"?

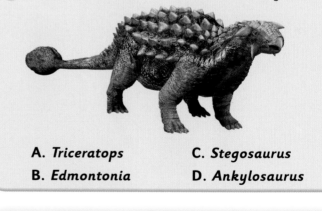

A. *Triceratops*   C. *Stegosaurus*
B. *Edmontonia*   D. *Ankylosaurus*

8 Which of these was one of the first marsupials?

A: *Mononykus*   B: *Docodon*
C: *Archelon*   D: *Alphadon*

9 *Mussaurus*, meaning "mouse lizard," was a...

A: Sauropod   B: Prosauropod
C: Theropod   D: Pterosaur

10 Which of these dinosaurs had three fingers on its forelimbs?

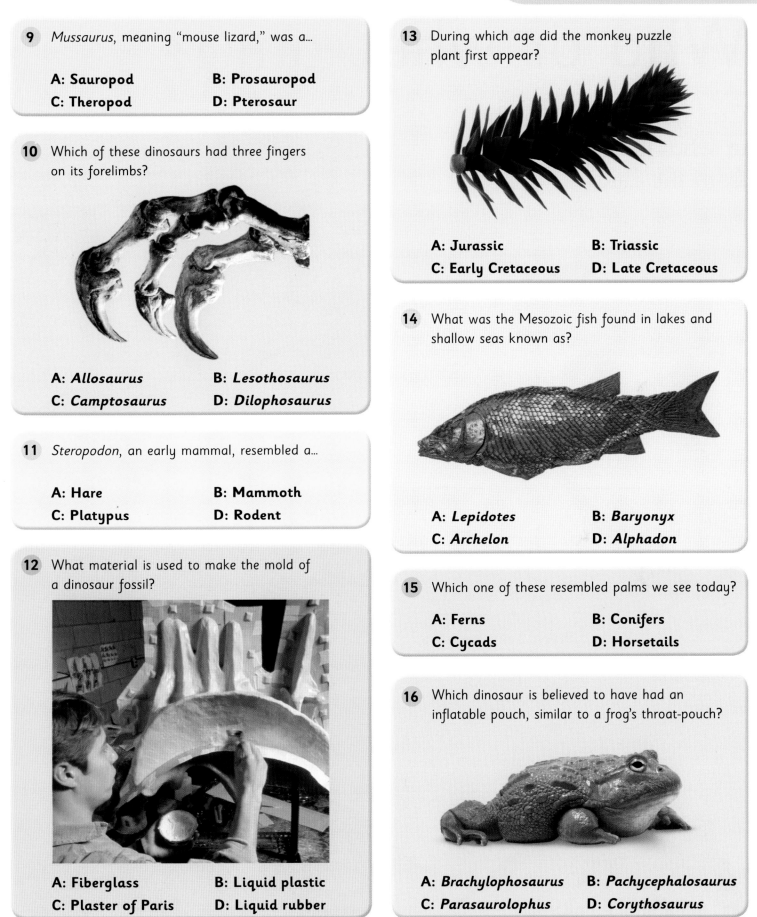

A: *Allosaurus*   B: *Lesothosaurus*
C: *Camptosaurus*   D: *Dilophosaurus*

11 *Steropodon*, an early mammal, resembled a...

A: Hare   B: Mammoth
C: Platypus   D: Rodent

12 What material is used to make the mold of a dinosaur fossil?

A: Fiberglass   B: Liquid plastic
C: Plaster of Paris   D: Liquid rubber

13 During which age did the monkey puzzle plant first appear?

A: Jurassic   B: Triassic
C: Early Cretaceous   D: Late Cretaceous

14 What was the Mesozoic fish found in lakes and shallow seas known as?

A: *Lepidotes*   B: *Baryonyx*
C: *Archelon*   D: *Alphadon*

15 Which one of these resembled palms we see today?

A: Ferns   B: Conifers
C: Cycads   D: Horsetails

16 Which dinosaur is believed to have had an inflatable pouch, similar to a frog's throat-pouch?

A: *Brachylophosaurus*   B: *Pachycephalosaurus*
C: *Parasaurolophus*   D: *Corythosaurus*

Answers: 1:C 2:B 3:A 4:A 5:C 6:C 7:D 8:D 9:B 10:A 11:C 12:D 13:B 14:A 15:C 16:A

Who or what am I?

Can you figure out who or what is being described from the clue?

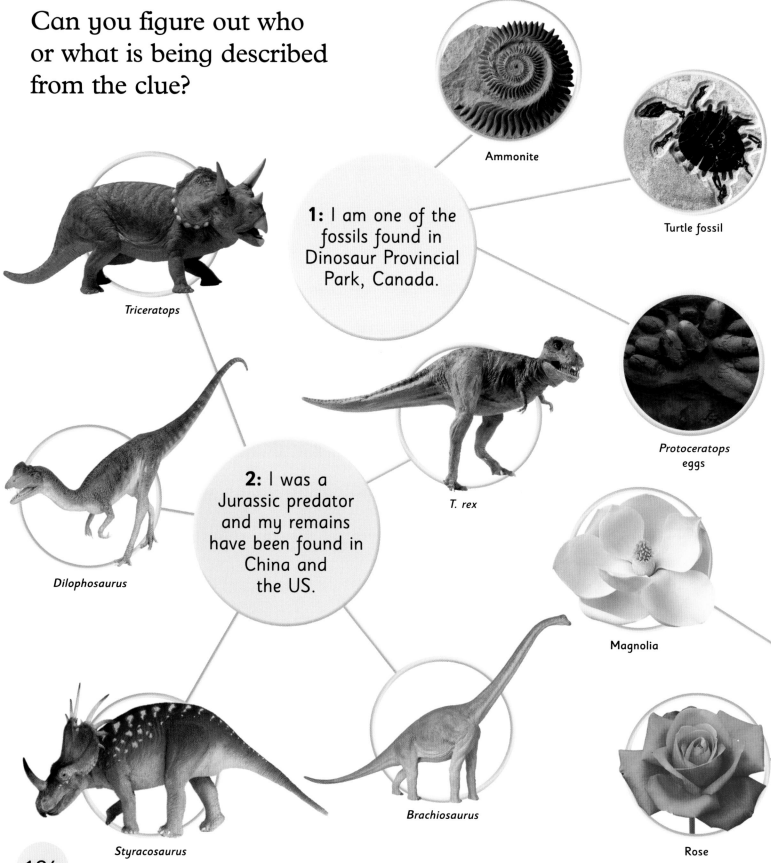

Ammonite

Turtle fossil

Triceratops

1: I am one of the fossils found in Dinosaur Provincial Park, Canada.

Protoceratops eggs

T. rex

Dilophosaurus

2: I was a Jurassic predator and my remains have been found in China and the US.

Magnolia

Brachiosaurus

Styracosaurus

Rose

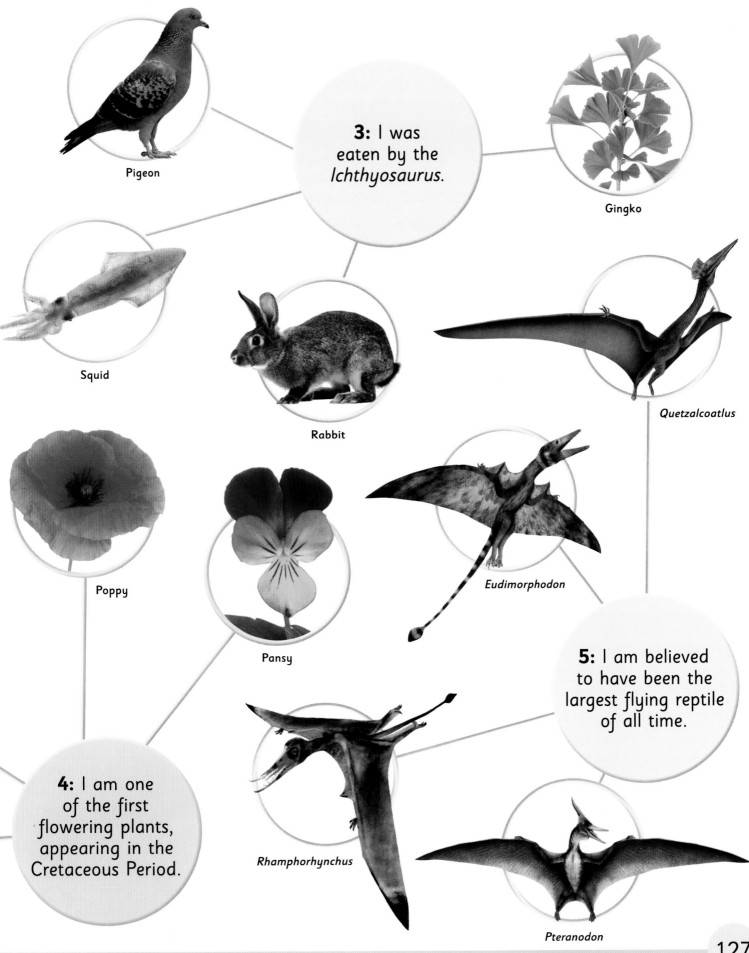

Pigeon

3: I was eaten by the *Ichthyosaurus.*

Gingko

Squid

Rabbit

Quetzalcoatlus

Poppy

Pansy

Eudimorphodon

5: I am believed to have been the largest flying reptile of all time.

4: I am one of the first flowering plants, appearing in the Cretaceous Period.

Rhamphorhynchus

Pteranodon

127

1: This dinosaur had about 120 teeth, and its nests have been found in Montana.

6: This was the first sauropod to be found. It lived by an ancient sea in an area now known as England.

2: This place in Arizona, North America, is packed with late Triassic fossils of plants and animals.

3: Fossils of hundreds of dinosaurs were found in this fossil quarry in New Mexico.

4: The near-complete skeleton of this dinosaur was found in 1988 near the Andes Mountains.

5: This massive dinosaur lived in the warm swamps of Cretaceous Argentina.

Where in the world?

Discover where the dinosaurs used to roam by matching the descriptions with the pictures.

Cetiosaurus

Ghost Ranch

Velociraptor skeleton

Vulcanodon

Gobi Desert

Yangchuanosaurus

7: Velociraptor 8: Gobi Desert 9: Yangchuanosaurus 10: Dryosaurus 11: Vulcanodon 12: Mamenchisaurus

7: The bones of this dog-sized dinosaur have been found in Asia.

8: This place is littered with the remains of the sheep-sized *Protoceratops*.

10: This dinosaur from eastern Africa had a parrotlike beak and leaf-shaped teeth.

9: This dinosaur, with the head the size of an armchair, hunted in Jurassic China.

11: This 21-ft (6.5-m) sauropod prowled Jurassic Zimbabwe.

12: This dinosaur was found in Australia. It is the longest-necked animal known to date.

Troodon   Mamenchisaurus   Herrerasaurus skeleton   Giganotosaurus   Petrified Forest   Dryosaurus

Answers: 1: *Troodon* 2: Petrified Forest 3: Ghost Ranch 4: *Herrerasaurus* 5: *Giganotosaurus* 6: *Cetiosaurus*

Glossary

archosaurs One of the group of animals that includes, or included, dinosaurs, birds, pterosaurs, and crocodiles

articulated Things that are joined together, such as the bones of a skeleton

cold-blooded Animal that cannot maintain its body temperature and has to rely on the Sun's heat to warm up or find shade in which to cool down. Reptiles are cold-blooded

geologist Scientist who studies the Earth and its rocks

habitat Place in which a group of animals and plants live. It could be a desert or a city park

herbivore Animal that only feeds on plants

Apatosaurus was a sauropod. It thrived 150 million years ago in the Jurassic period.

continent Large area of land, such as Africa

coprolite Fossilized dinosaur droppings

Cretaceous Geological name given to the period between 145 and 66 million years ago

cynodont Carnivorous, mammal-like reptile that was the immediate ancestor of mammals

extinction Dying out of an animal or plant species

fossil Remains of animal or plant matter that have been preserved in the Earth's crust

Jurassic Geological name given to the period between 201 and 145 million years ago

mammal Warm-blooded animal that has a backbone and produces milk to feed its young

Mesozoic Era Major division of geological time (called an era) when the dinosaurs lived. It contains the Triassic, Jurassic, and Cretaceous periods

meteorite Lump of rock that falls to the Earth from space

nocturnal Animal that is active at night and sleeps during the day

paleontologist Scientist who removes animal and plant fossils from the ground and studies them

predator Animal that hunts and kills other animals for food

prey Animal that is hunted and eaten by another animal

theropod Group name for meat-eating dinosaurs

trace fossil Fossil that indicates where an animal has been, but is not part of the animal's remains. Fossilized footprints are trace fossils

Triassic Geological name given to the period between 252 and 201 million years ago

tsunami Huge wave caused by movements in the Earth's crust. The cause, for example, may be a deep-sea earthquake

warm-blooded Animal that can maintain its body temperature by using food as fuel to generate heat. Humans are warm-blooded

vertebra One of the bones that link together to form an animal's backbone, or spine

reptile One of the group of animals that includes turtles, lizards, crocodiles, snakes, pterosaurs, and dinosaurs

sauropod Name for a group of large, plant-eating dinosaurs. Sauropods had long necks and tails and bulky bodies

scavenger Animal that feeds on the dead bodies of other animals

species Group of those living things that share the same characteristics and breed with others of the same type

Dracorex hogwartsia

The name of this newly discovered dinosaur was inspired by the dragons from the *Harry Potter* novels.

131

Index

Can you recognize and name any of the dinosaur silhouettes? Turn to the next page to check your answers.

How many dinosaurs on the previous page did you manage to name?

Plateosaurus

Thecodontosaurus

Poekilopleuron

Compsognathus

Brachiosaurus

Stegosaurus

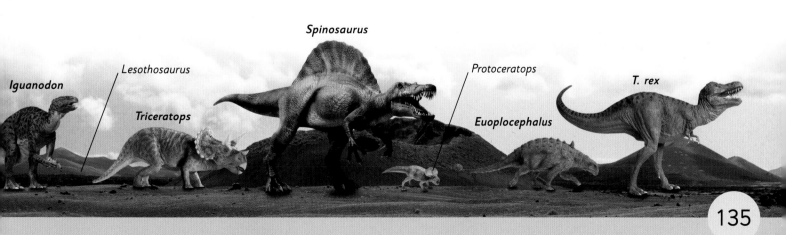

Iguanodon

Lesothosaurus

Triceratops

Spinosaurus

Protoceratops

Euoplocephalus

T. rex

Picture credits

The publisher would like to thank the following for their kind permission to reproduce their photographs:

(Key: a-above; b-below/bottom; c-centre; l-left; r-right; t-top)

Alamy Images: Jeff Morgan 72b; Werner Otto 126b, 127b; **American Museum Of Natural History**: 47c, 87tl; **Ardea**: Francois Gohier 22br, 58cr, 59cr; **Corbis**: Macduff Everton 129br; Reuters 124cra; Michael S. Yamashita 125cla; Gary Bell 90-91c; Bettmann 46tl; Jonathan Blair 33tr, 36-37bc; Gary Braasch 80-81bc; James D'Addio / Beateworks 10tr; Terry W. Eggers 37crb; Sandy Felsenthal 1bl; Darrell Gulin 14tc; Wolfgang Kaehler 80cl; Layne Kennedy 76cl, 107clb; Macduff Everton 47tl; Charles Mauzy 46ca; Richard T. Nowitz 106cb; Greg Probst 66-67bc; Louie Psihoyos 22cl, 22cr, 26tr, 39br, 41tl, 67cra, 68tr, 77tr; Reuters 77br; Reuters / Peter Morgan 54cr; ML Sinibaldi 62-63c (background); Jon Sparks 38tr; Jim Zuckerman 51tr; **DK Images**: American Museum of Natural History 20fcra, 21ca; Angus Beare 113cl; Simone Boni/L.R. Galante 70fcl; Centaur Studios 7fbr, 12fcla, 20tc; Centaur Studios/Andy Crawford 126fbr; Peter Chadwick 35fbr, 84fbl, 85br; Jim Channell 120ftr; Brian Cosgrove 37tc; Bedrock Studios 4bl, 5bl, 19fcr, 39fcl, 57tc, 57bl, 78fbl, 120fcrb, 126fbl; Courtesy of Dinosaur State Park, Connecticut 101fbl; Courtesy of the |Natural History Museum, London 6868fcl; Courtesy of the American Museum of Natural History 68fcl, 73fcrb, 108ftr, 108fbl, 108fbr, 109fbl, 109fbr, 110ftr, 110fclb, 111fcra, 111fcl; Courtesy of the Carnegie Museum of Natural History, Pittsburgh 123fcl; Courtesy of the Field Museum, Chicago 65bc; Courtesy of the Institute of Geology and Palaeontology, Tubingen, Germany 39fcr; Courtesy of the Museo Arentino De Cirendas Naterales, Buenos Aires 75ca; Courtesy of The National Birds of Prey Centre, Gloucestershire 113fcrb, 117fcr; Courtesy of the National Museum of Natural History, Smithsonian Institution 57ftl; Courtesy of the Natural History Museum, London 11bl, 13fcrb, 15fcr, 113cla, 119cla, 120fcr; Courtesy of the Natural History Museum, London / Colin Keates 15c, 18fcl, 21cla; Courtesy of Peter Minister, Digital Sculptor 4-5c, 15crb, 28fcl, 69cl, 75cl; Courtesy of the Royal Tyrell Museum 13fbr; Courtesy of the Royal Tyrrell Museum of Palaeontology, Alberta 65fcr; Courtesy of the Royal Tyrrell Museum of Palaeontology, Alberta, Canada 75fcr, 120fclb; Courtesy of The Sedgewick Museum of Geology, Cambridge 101fcl; Courtesy of the Senckenberg Nature Museum, Frankfurt 65br, 118bl; Courtesy of the State Museum of Nature, Stuttgart 33fcrb, 65fcrb, 105fcra; James Stevenson 19br; Roby Braun 4fbr, 12cb, 17fcr, 17ftr, 73cl, 121cr, 126bc, 126br, 127fbl; Courtsey of Royal Tyrell Museum 69fclb;

Andy Crawford 16, 39cla; Dave King 20tl, 120fcra; David Donkin 9bl, 9br; Donks Models 11ftr; Christine M. Douglas 45ftr, 57fbr; Philip Dowell 10fbl, 10bl, 22bl; Mike Dunning 11fcrb; Neil Fletcher / Matthew Ward 57fcra; Giuliano Fornari 114cra, 114crb; Christopher & Sally Gable 25bc; Steve Gorton 57fcrb; Steve Gorton / John Holmes 74cb, 75clb; Jonathan Hateley 27fcl, 113fcra, 118cr, 119clb; Nigel Hicks 11fbr; Graham High, Centaur Studios 4br, 5fbl, 12c, 29bc, 68bc, 69bc, 114cr, 126crb, 127bl, 127br; John Holmes 25ftl, 29fcr; Jon Hughes 34-35b, 35tl, 43tr, 44-45c, 53cr, 56c, 57b, 60c, 61r, 63c, 79cr, 88-89c; Jeremy Hunt 95fcr; Colin Keates 101cla, 101cb; Colin Keates / Courtesy of The Natural History Museum, London 31fcr, 31fcrb, 54cra, 56ftr; Colin Keates / Natural History Museum, London 17fcrb; Gary Kevin 24fcrb, 25fcrb; Gunter Marx 113clb; Ray Moller 10fcl; Frank Greenaway 11br, 14, 95ftr, 95fcrb, 116ca, 116c, 116cb; Natural History Museum, London 24fbl, 29fbr, 31fcra; Stepehen Oliver 99br; Gary Ombler 4bc, 20tr, 27fbl, 63cra, 71crb, 79fcl, 99fcra, 119cb, 127fbr; Gary Ombler; Lloyd Park 59tc, 117fbl; Peabody Museum of Natural History, Yale University 84fclb, 85tc; Peabody Museum of Natural History, Yale University / Lynton Gardiner 84bl; David Peart 116fcl; Miguel Periera 45bc; Roger Phillips 38fbl, 43fcra; Luis Rey 84tl, 84ftl; Rough guides 15ftr, 127c; Karl Shone 113fcr, 116fbl; Steve Shott 95fcra; Staab Studios 120fbl; John Temperton 55fcra, 56fcra, 121crb; Cecile Treal & Jean-Michel Ruiz 11fcr; Matthew Ward 32fcla, 41ftr, 53fcrb; Laura Wickenden 117ftl; James Young 71ftr; Jerry Young 11cr (Scrubland), 14cl, 20cra, 113fbr, 117fclb; **Dorling Kindersley**: Peter Minister 1c; American Museum of Natural History 125bl; Bedrock Studios 129bc (Giganotosaurus), 129fbr; Roby Braun 122ca; Neil Fletcher 127tl; Jon Hughes 124crb, 127cr, 127bc, 128br, 128fbr, 129bl; Instituto Fundacion Miguel Lillo, Argentina 129bc; **Dreamstime.com**: Leonello Calvetti 123t, Christineg 128br (Desert); **FLPA**: Flip de Nooyer / Foto Natura 119tr, 119tc; **Fotolia**: Michael Rosskothen 120crb; **Getty Images**: 77c; AFP / William West 61tl; Theo Allofs 60-61cb (background); Jack Dvkinga 34bc; Rich Frishman 107br; David Hiser 64bl; Brian Kenney 21clb; Raimund Koch 38tl (Background); Timothy Laman / National Geographic 27ca; Klaus Nigge 78-79c (background); Panoramic Images 42l, 43cr, 55c, 68-69bc; Louie Psihoyos 105tl, 105crb, 106cra,

107tl, 120cr, 121c; James Randklev 40-41t; Scott Sady 28-29tc; Miguel Salmeron 26-27bc; Science Faction / Louie Psihoyos 64, 100b, 103t; Pankai & Insy Shah 26-27 (wadi); Andreas Stirnberg 48-49c; Hans Strand 82l, 83br; Steffen Thalemann 44-45b; Nobumichi Tamura / Stocktrek Images 128fbl; **Karen Carr**: 35br; **Kokoro Dinosaurs**: 2-3, 119br, 120bc; **The Natural History Museum, London**: 5br, 6tl, 6cl, 6-7bc, 13crb, 18br, 19cb, 20cr, 21cl, 23bc, 24cl, 25cra, 27tl, 32bl, 67br, 83tl, 88tr, 89c, 120clb, 120cl, 120cla, 120fbl; Anness Publishing 120fcla, 120fcl; De Agostini 54tr; **NHPA / Photoshot**: Andrea & Antonella Ferrari 70-71cb; Jonathan & Angela Scott 34clb; **OSF / photolibrary**: 88cl; Highlights for Children 40bl, 45tc, 45tr; **Reuters**: Peter Morgan 97tc; Ho New 97ca; **Science Faction Images**: Louie Psihoyos 13cra, 18bl, 22cl (background), 23cr, 23tl, 24cra, 31tl, 42clb, 50-51bc, 53tl, 67cr, 79bl, 84-85c, 98cl; **Science Photo Library**: Hervé Conge, ISM 69tl, 126cra; Christian Darkin 8c, 13cla, 30tr, 30-31c, 73t, 97cla; Bernhard Edmaier 115cr; Carlos Goldin 78tr; Gary Hincks 36-37ca; NASA 114bc; Laurie O'Keefe 50clb; David Parker 76-77c; D. Van Ravensway 114clb; Joe Tucciarone 86cr; **Mineo Shiraishi**: 53c, 81b; **Still Pictures**: Kelvin Aitken 86l; John Cancalosi / Peter Arnold. Inc. 1cl, 23tc; **SuperStock**: J. Silver 21br; **The Children's Museum of Indianapolis**: 123br; CM Studio: 1r, 34cl, 36tl, 42-43c, 55cr, 57cra, 59tr, 81tr, 126bl, 128; **Tom Dempsey / www.photoseek. com**: 48-49t; **US Geological Survey Western Region**: 11cl; **Special Collections Department**, J. Willard Marriott Library, University of Utah: 65tl; **Warren Photographic**: 32-33, 72t, 112-113c, 116tr; Jane Burton 94bc; **Kevin Wasden (kevinwasden. com)**: 53cb; **Yale University Peabody Museum Of Natural History**: 99tl
Additional photography by Andy Crawford: 71ct, 82-83 (Troodon models), 88tc, 89tr, 105tl

All other images © Dorling Kindersley
For further information see:
www.dkimages.com

Acknowledgments

Dorling Kindersley would like to thank:
Tim Batty, The Dinosaur Museum, Dorchester, (www.thedinosaurmuseum.com) for all his help, Penny Smith, Fleur Star, Lorrie Mack, and Carrie Love for editorial assistance and Gemma Fletcher and Hedi Gutt for design assistance. Thank you also to Dougal Dixon for his patience and for allowing photography of his models of Troodon.

Eoraptor, a turkey-sized dinosaur that lived in the Triassic period